America and the
Mythology of Greatness

America and the Mythology of Greatness

By Joseph Aprile

iUniverse, Inc.

New York Lincoln Shanghai

America and the Mythology of Greatness

iUniverse, Inc.

For information address:
iUniverse, Inc.
2021 Pine Lake Road, Suite 100
Lincoln, NE 68512
www.iuniverse.com

Cover graphic depicts Seattle anti-war protestors carrying images from Pablo Picasso's famous work entitled, "Guernica."

ISBN: 0-595-32691-9

Printed in the United States of America

For my partner and life's companion, Julia Chase, whose patience and generous assistance has made this book possible.

Contents

Introduction

America of the twenty-first century finds itself involved in a so-called War against Terrorism as a consequence of the devastating attack against the World Trade towers in New York and the Pentagon on September 11, 2001. The rhetoric used by the administration of George W. Bush conceives of the war as a battle between the forces of good and evil. This is certainly not a new rationale for a nation in times of war. It has been used repeatedly during America's numerous military actions since the inception of the republic.

It is quite astonishing how this shallow, self-serving and specious analysis is so readily accepted by the majority of the general population. There is a fabulous myth of America's historical greatness that colors and shadows everything that the nation does in the world. It is the blind acceptance of this mythology that ensures that the imperious and arrogant behavior of the world's only superpower will persist and guarantee the continuation of a world order that aligns itself with a very small minority of the prosperous and wages economic warfare against the overwhelmingly and desperately poor who represent a majority of the world's people.

These times are particularly ominous for a number of reasons. The United States is now the only superpower with a vast stockpile of weapons of mass destruction; the only nation that has ever used nuclear weapons against civilian populations, and currently plans to develop a family of small nuclear weapons designed to be used against hardened targets. The government is also involved in a remarkably expensive military expansion that will further dwarf the military weaponry of even its wealthiest allies. A part of that expansion represents the militarization of space. The world has a lot to be concerned about especially since the cadre of the powerful in government (the likes of Donald

1

Rumsfeld, Richard Perl and Paul Wolfewitz) are urging an unabash-edly imperial policy that would threaten all potential foes with deadly and pervasive force.

This view has been detailed in a new National Security Policy that has been promulgated by the George W. Bush administration. I believe this to be a very dangerous document in terms of the kind of precedent it is setting in regard to the basis of foreign policy in the United States. The central theme of this policy is, "While the United States will con-stantly strive to enlist the support of the international community, we will not hesitate to act alone, if necessary, to exercise our right of self-defense by acting preemptively against such terrorists...." This world view stands against major covenants of international law. It will open the door for nations throughout the world to strike out at their ene-mies based on a perceived threat. It effectively attempts to legitimize the use of overwhelming force against adversaries as a major compo-nent of foreign policy. It is the behavior of a powerful rogue state pro-claiming itself to be above and outside the community of nations in which it lives, and, as such, it is a policy that must be repudiated.

This country has purposefully shown by its past behavior in Iraq that it is quite capable of destroying the infrastructure of any nation it considers a threat, leaving great suffering in its wake without even the faintest recognition of the consequence of its actions. The world has grown fearful, distrustful and resentful of this brutish giant in its midst.

The U.S. Congress has remained passive in the wake of this momentous change in policy as it has with the passage of the Patriot Act. The passage of the Uniting and Strengthening America by Provid-ing Appropriate Tools Required to Intercept and Obstruct Terrorism Act (USA Patriot Act) has legitimized levels of surveillance into the pri-vate lives of individuals and organizations that have seriously impacted civil liberties in the United States. The act was passed hurriedly under significant pressure from Attorney General John Ashcroft, who warned of imminent terrorist attacks if they were not thwarted by the provi-sions of this legislation. The Congress caved in under this intense pressure and essentially abrogated its obligation to debate such a profoundly important issue, a behavior reminiscent of the passage of the Gulf of Tonkin Resolution that ushered in the debacle that was the Vietnam War.

This act has undermined aspects of the First, Fourth, Fifth and Sixth amendments to the Constitution. The provisions in the act range from the FBI's enhanced policies of search and surveillance to the indefinite detention of both citizens and non-citizens without formal charges and access to counsel. Furthermore, provisions of this law threaten the right to dissent, a crucially important right in any government that claims itself to be a true democracy. The right to dissent can be effectively compromised by the threat of the possibility of harassment by investigators, by allowing searches on little evidence and by creating the risk of felony prosecution for minor criminal violations.

Indicative of just how tenuous our supposed liberties are in the eyes of the law, Supreme Court Justice Antonin Scalia was reported to have made the following comment at John Carroll University, "Most of the rights you enjoy go way beyond what the Constitution requires" because "the Constitution just set minimums." He went on to say that in wartime, "The protections will be ratcheted down to the constitutional minimum."

In his book entitled, *All the Laws but One: Civil Liberties in Wartime*, the Chief Justice of the United States, William Rehnquist, claimed that the, "Constitution has not greatly bothered any wartime president." When these sentiments are juxtaposed with the stated belief that the war against terrorism will be fought for many years into the future, the curtailment of liberties may, in fact, become permanent.

The following is taken from a piece entitled, *The State of Civil Liberties a Year Later*, by the Center for Constitutional Rights. "The USA Patriot Act contains provisions that will chill or even criminalize peoples' legitimate expressions of their political views. For example, the Act creates a new category of crime, domestic terrorism, which blurs the line between speech and criminal activity. Section 802 of the Act defines domestic terrorism as "acts dangerous to human life that are a violation of criminal laws that appear to be intended to influence the policy of a government by intimidation or coercion." This definition is so vague that acts of civil disobedience may be construed to violate the law. Civil disobedience typically seeks to influence government policy, and therefore may be construed as an attempt to coerce that change. Furthermore, the portion of the definition stating that acts must be "dangerous to human life" is extremely broad: it does not distinguish between intentional acts and those that cause inadvertent harm....Such a broad definition invites abuse."

The mythology of greatness, that is used to buttress these policies, needs to be discredited if any human progress is to be expected. It is time for the nation and its people to begin to honestly evaluate its behavior, take responsibility for its actions and, most importantly, change them. The insecurity and violence that plagues humanity has its roots in severe poverty, economic inequality and social injustice. If there is to be hope for the future, the political, social and economic imbalances between the rich and poor nations must be corrected.

The American people find themselves at a significant crossroads. If they remain silent, they can only expect to find themselves living in a far more dangerous world than the one in which they are now living. It has already become quite clear that a majority of the citizenry do not accept the idea that the behavior of the United States in the world may have contributed substantially to the events of September 11. They prefer to see themselves as victims of evil powers that envy us our freedom. Most importantly, they seem willing to sacrifice personal liberties in order to feel "safer." Americans have become afraid and uncertain, and it is the government that is exploiting this fear. The policies and behavior that the leadership is following will, in fact, make Americans far more vulnerable especially when they venture far from their own borders.

It is only through concerted and persistent effort that the nation can be made to change course and avoid the abyss we are all heading for. If generations to come are to see a meaningful future, we must insist on a change in the way we see ourselves and our place in the world. The veils of myth and self-delusion must be lifted so that we might collectively regain our sanity. Preserving our privileged place in the world through brutal force and the threat of force may succeed in the short term, but is bound to fail over time.

1

The Myths of Democracy and Freedom

All empires have fantastic stories regarding their origins. The Romans had their tale about Romulus and Remus, the alleged founders of Rome. The ancient Egyptians had their creation stories as well as the Mayans and the Incas.

The creation story of the United States is, of course, more contemporary than these examples, although, in some ways, still as fantastic. The story tells us that our great leaders (George Washington, Thomas Jefferson, Alexander Hamilton, James Madison, etc) came together and crafted the Declaration of Independence and Constitution that detailed the creation of a democratic republic by and for all the people and established the rules of governance that would ensure its continued existence. According to this view, they went on to implement a structure of government that would preserve democracy and freedom for present and future generations. This version of events is familiar to everyone who went through the public school system.

The historic record, of course, supports this sequence of events. The authors of these documents were motivated by a desire to rid the colonialists of their domination by the British. There was a thoughtful and considered attempt to establish a representative form of government with a system of checks and balances that effectively separated the executive, legislative and judicial arms of government into separate branches.

It is the intent of the founders, however, that is open to question. They were primarily concerned with creating a stable government and avoiding the social chaos so prevalent in many parts of Europe at the time. As stated by Alexander Hamilton in the *Federalist Papers* (The Federalist No. 9, November 21, 1787), "A Firm Union will be of the utmost moment to the peace and liberty of the States, as a barrier against domestic faction and insurrection. It is impossible to read the history of the petty republics of Greece and Italy without feeling sensations of horror and disgust at the distractions with which they were continually agitated, and at the rapid succession of revolutions by which they were kept in a state of perpetual vibration between the extremes of tyranny and anarchy...."

The founding fathers, all male, white and propertied, had no intention of allowing the masses to have the power to shape their own lives and destiny. They sought to create structures that would, in fact, retain power in the hands of the wealthy. In that era, before the ascendance of capital, wealth was measured in terms of property. It was the white propertied males who were to have the franchise and controlling interest in government. As Kevin Phillips has described in his book entitled, *Wealth and Democracy*, many of the affluent white males made their fortunes in war profiteering. "In 1780, men with privateering and war supply connections were climbing into the upper ranks. By 1784 they were moving toward the top. And by 1790 they were the Boston elite."

The founders did not trust the people, and in many ways held them in disdain and were fearful of the possibility of popular revolt against the domination by the powerful. There were already instances of popular uprisings demonstrating the disparity between rich and poor. Howard Zinn addresses this issue in his masterful book, *A People's History of the United States*. An examination of the tax lists in Boston in the early 1770's showed that 5 percent of the wealthiest taxpayers controlled 49 percent of the taxable assets. Similar inequities could be found in Philadelphia and New York. Members of the lower classes began to use the Boston town meetings to air their frustrations. This made the wealthy nervous. Some of these accumulated feelings may have contributed to the mob action following the Stamp Act of 1765. In Philadelphia, there was a strong movement against the wealthy and the right to unlimited private property. The countryside was not immune to this antipathy against wealth. Rebellions took place among the farmers in the Hudson Valley, Vermont and North Carolina. In Orange County, North Carolina, the Regulator movement was conceived. This movement was organized to prevent tax collection and the taking of property on account of delinquent taxes.

These are some examples that demonstrate the extent to which there existed an inequitable distribution of wealth even before the British were successfully driven out of the colonies. The wealthy were not only represented by the British, but also by nationalists. This inequality did not disappear following the revolution. The wealth was transferred from the British and loyalists to those who were already in a position of power in the colonies.

The traditional view of the Constitution is that of a document that established the creation of a society that was freed of inequality and opened to rule by the people. The idea that the founders may have been motivated by concerns other than freedom and democracy when framing the Constitution has been put forward by Charles Beard in this book, *An Economic Interpretation of the Constitution*. Beard studied the economic background of the fifty-five men who gathered to draft the Constitution. He found that a majority was lawyers and men of wealth and property with a vested interest in maintaining the economic preeminence of themselves and their class. They had a good reason to create a strong central government i.e. to retain and maintain the property relations of the dominant class of which they were members. The need for a strong central government to ensure the safety and protection of the powerful economic interests was dramatized by Shay's rebellion of 1787. A serious depression had struck the farmers of Western Massachusetts. Farmers who were unable to pay their debts often found themselves in jail. Those most seriously impacted, felt they were being victimized by the mercantile elite of Eastern Massachusetts, who demanded hard currency to pay foreign creditors. The frustrated farmers reacted with an armed uprising which began as petitions to the government for paper currency, lower taxes and legal reform. They attacked the Court of Common Pleas at Northampton. Other courts were also targeted with the hope of preventing further trials and imprisonment of debtors. The leader of the rebellion was Daniel Shays, a veteran of the Revolution. The Supreme Judicial Court responded by indicting eleven of the leaders of sedition. The Massachusetts governor, James Bowdoin, put General Benjamin Lincoln in charge of a force of militia. The rebellion was squelched and fourteen of the leaders of the rebellion including Shay were sentenced to death. In the words of Chief Justice William Cushing, "[I fear] evil minded persons, leaders of the insurgents…[waging war] against the Commonwealth, to bring the whole government and all the good people of this state, if not continent, under absolute command and subjugation to one or two ignorant, unprincipled, bankrupt, desperate individuals." Many of these individuals were later pardoned, however. Some historians feel that Shay's rebellion brought social unrest into such sharp focus that it was one of the leading impetuses for the creation of the Constitution of the United States.

There are additional and more contemporary instances of popular unrest I would like to allude to: the Haymarket Affair (May 1, 1886) and the assassination of Fred Hampton of the Black Panther Party (December 4, 1969).

On May 1, 1886, 340,000 workers went on strike all over the country demanding an eight hour day. In the city of Chicago, 80,000 workers took to the streets. Anarchist militants were among those who were instrumental in organizing this workers' action. The following day, the Chicago police were mobilized against the strikers at the McCormick Harvester Works. They fired on the crowd killing six strikers. The next day a protest rally was held at Haymarket Square. The police attempted to break up the rally, and in the chaos a bomb was thrown at the police killing one and fatally wounding seven others.

The subsequent trial sentenced five anarchists to death. Four were later hung (Albert Parsons, August Spies, George Engel and Adolph Fishcer), and one of the condemned (Louis Lingg) committed suicide. Seven years after the hangings, a judicial enquiry found all the executed were innocent of the charges and three serving life sentences were released. In the years that followed, the growing labor movement had to struggle against their corporate employers and both the Federal and local governments in order to curtail some of the horrible abuses perpetrated against employees, and secure decent living conditions for working people.

The 1960s saw the rise of the civil rights movement. The leaders of this movement spanned the political spectrum from the non-violent civil disobedience advocated by Dr. Martin Luther King Jr. to the more radical ideology of the Black Panthers, and were seen as serious threats to the establishment. The strategy of character assassination taken against Dr. King by the FBI has been well documented. It was an unscrupulous attempt to discredit the man's ideas by exposing details of his personal life. Thankfully, it did not succeed. A far more drastic strategy, however, was perpetrated against the more radical Black Panthers. On the morning of December 4, 1969, a heavily armed contingent of the Chicago Police stormed into the apartment of Fred Hampton, fiery spokesman for the Black Panther Party, killing him and Mark Clark and wounding many others. The police and State Attorney Hanrahan claimed self-defense. Ensuing investigations demonstrated that over 200 bullets were fired by the police and only 4 could be attributed to the occupants of the apartment. It ultimately came to light, through documents released under the Freedom of Information Act, that the FBI, in collusion with the Chicago Police, had planned the assassination of Fred Hampton under the umbrella of the Counter Intelligence Program of the Federal Bureau of Investigation (Cointelpro). Cointelpro was begun in 1967 by the Director of the FBI, J. Edgar Hoover. Cointelpro used many tactics to undermine and destroy what was deemed radical and dangerous groups. Hoover determined Fred Hampton to be very dangerous to the security of the United States. For this reason, plans were formulated to eliminate this perceived threat.

These examples demonstrate the level of distrust and apprehension that the men in power have felt regarding the general population, and clearly show what lengths they will go to contain popular discontent and to insure that their power remains intact.

This type of behavior does not reflect democratic principles. Democracy is, "A government in which the supreme power is vested in the people." If democracy was, indeed, alive, it would be hard to envision the current institutions and policies of government that so often act contrary to the public will. I propose that it is, in fact, a democracy for the wealthy. Native Americans were certainly not viewed as belonging under the umbrella of democracy. Quite to the contrary, they were seen as sub-human and worthy of removal from their lands for the purpose of westward expansion of the white settlers. They were, in fact, exterminated to accomplish this "ethnic cleansing." The native population was estimated to have been between ten and fourteen million before colonialization and is now about four million in number. It should not be forgotten that while all the high-sounding democratic ideals were being proclaimed, the slave trade continued unabated. Slavery was seen as an economic and political necessity, especially for the Southern white plantation owners. The human cost in suffering and death that resulted from slavery is incalculable. The country remains in denial of much of its barbaric past to this day. History is replete with evidence that democracy was not intended for the blacks, for the Native Americans, for women or for the vast majority of whites without land and left at the mercy of the white men of wealth and power.

The actual history as seen through the eyes of the players themselves is quite unambiguous in this regard. It paints a picture of oppression and brutality that is well documented and has been recently compiled in, *A People's History of the United States* to mention one important source. Yet the myth remains as strong as ever. No one wishes to see themselves and their lives as controlled by others. Unlike the blacks whose enslavement was an undeniable fact, whites perceive themselves as among the chosen and, therefore, worthy of all the fruits and benefits of democracy. To see themselves otherwise would be unsettling.

The perception that democracy is alive and well is bolstered by the machinery of propaganda. Two important channels through which propaganda operates are the education of the nation's children and the messages conveyed by the privately owned media through their news and information agencies. The curriculum of the schools in terms of the teaching of American history and politics is ripe with mis-information, distortions and outright lies. Simply reflect on what you have been taught about American history in the lower grades, high school and even in higher institutions. Where in the school texts can you find unabashed references to the extent of the genocide of the Native American populations, a detailed look at the brutal and sadistic mechanisms and practices of slavery, the oppression and violence perpetrated against immigrant populations and organized worker movements, and the blatant use of so-called "weapons of mass destruction" against defenseless civilian populations throughout the world under the spurious guise of war, national defense and security?

This same avoidance of uncomfortable truth is also remarkably evident in what we refer to as the free press. The press has come increasingly under the control of corporate conglomerates, global in scope and beholding to no one except their own interests. Journalists pay hollow lip service to objectivity and the uncovering of truth especially if that truth questions the political agenda. It is primarily due to the exceptional and courageous coverage of world events by the alternative media that American readers have been provided with a glimpse into the real consequences of international and domestic policy formulated by administrations and legislative bodies that have become dependent upon financial contributions from corporate interests.

Legislators have grown dependent upon the largess of corporate contributors. Not unlike the makeup of the Congress at the founding of the nation, it is the wealthy and privileged who reach and hold office. According to a 1996 survey, 39 percent of U.S. Senators had a net worth in excess of one million dollars with some members being extraordinarily wealthy. Whose interests might you suppose the wealthy would be most likely to support and further? The answer, of course, becomes quite evident when the kinds of legislation that are proposed and passed are examined. Why is it that the interests of the energy, defense, mining, timber and pharmaceutical industries are well represented by legislation, while those of labor, the poor and the dispossessed are not? Why is it that so much legislation that embodies the wishes of the people like an adequate national health care system, public transportation, affordable housing and support of a living wage consistently fails to pass? The voice of the few who have money is readily heard, while the collective voices of those without are essentially ignored.

We call ourselves a democracy. How is this democracy practiced? Is it truly a democracy of the people? Let us begin by looking at the most often referred to expression of democracy: the right to vote. An examination of the voting process clearly demonstrates how undemocratic a process it is. The political landscape is controlled by two major parties that insure their own predominance. One way they do this is to make sure that the televised presidential debates are only represented by the major parties with few exceptions (the candidacy of Ross Perot being one example). This was made abundantly clear by the exclusion of Ralph Nader from the debates in election 2000. The rationale for this exclusion is that in order for a candidate to participate in the nationally televised debates, he or she must have a minimum of 15 percent of popular support as determined by the polls. How can a candidate get public support if unable to reach a wide audience in the first place? Without this national coverage, major third party candidates have a nearly impossible task of getting the exposure they need to launch a successful campaign. The election campaigns themselves are tightly controlled media events that assiduously avoid discussion and debate around the critical issues that face the nation such as health care, education, homelessness, poverty, the prison system, housing, campaign finance reform, military spending, foreign policy, etc. The campaigns rely on the media through news coverage and political ads to reduce all issues to sound bites, slogans and demagoguery. In addition, these ads are exorbitantly expensive. The end result is the selection of candidates with the largest cache of campaign contributions and, therefore, beholding to the powerful corporate interests. It is, in fact, a democracy for the powerful in keeping with the system that our forefathers always envisioned. It has become an inherently corrupt system dependent upon the affluent for sustenance.

Regardless of these deficiencies, we have always prided ourselves on the ultimate fairness of the vote. This, as well, has been put into serious question on account of the questionable decision by the Supreme Court to allow the electoral votes from Florida to go towards George W. Bush in the 2000 presidential election. This decision was made in spite of the numerous questions surrounding the counting of those ballots and wholesale discrimination at the polls especially towards African Americans through the use of fraudulent felony lists that effectively purged many law abiding voters from the polls. The details surrounding these events will be examined in greater depth in Chapter Six of this book. In this way, the Supreme Court subverted the will of the people in favor of a candidate who failed to get a majority of the votes nationwide.

Evidence of the existence of an oligarchy (the power which a few citizens of a state have usurped, which ought, by the constitution, to reside in the people) rather than a truly representative democracy is embodied in the fact that members of Congress, the judicial and executive branches, invariably wealthy themselves, are indebted to the wealthy and that their agendas naturally reflect, reinforce and support that wealth. The corporate hold on the Federal government is so pervasive that the voice of the people has become effectively muted. The influence of corporate interests is directed through lobbyists who represent them. As reported by the Wall Street Journal in an article dated June 19, 1996, the number of lobbyists that inundate the Congress during legislative sessions is said to number over 67,000 with an average annual salary of $547,000. It is further estimated that there are about 125 lobbyists per congressman. Lobbying represents an industry that generates more than $8.4 billion dollars annually, as of 1996.

Another telling piece of evidence is that the agencies that were supposedly created to protect the health and well being of the general population, support the moneyed special interests, and that the members of these agencies ultimately work for the very corporations that they are supposed to regulate. Examples are the Security and Exchange Commission, the Department of the Interior, the Federal Trade Commission, the Federal Drug Agency, the Energy Department, etc. For the purpose of example, I would like to examine the Department of Energy in some detail to demonstrate the extent to which the system is corrupted by corporate power and influence.

The George W. Bush administration appointed Vice President Dick Cheney to head a task force for the purpose of submitting a plan to "reform" the nation's energy policy. In doing so, the Vice President held secret meetings with oil corporation representatives. It must be kept in mind that Dick Cheney was the chief executive officer (CEO) of Halliburton, the leading oil developer in the world. Dick Cheney was committed in his refusal to reveal the participants of these meetings, claiming executive privilege. This is an interesting argument given that the officers of government are supposed to be working for the people. Do not the people have a right to know just how public policy is crafted? This is just additional evidence that supports the idea that, at best, we have a token democracy.

The Department of Energy reluctantly produced a list of thirty-nine business executives and lobbyists who met with Department of Energy Secretary Spencer Abraham to discuss the task force efforts. As of March, 2002, documents have revealed additional meetings and identified sixty-four additional executives and lobbyists who met with the Secretary while the energy plan was being written. These additional interested parties had contributed 22.6 million dollars through individual Political Action Committees (PAC) and soft money contributions to federal candidates since 1999. Over 17 million dollars of that total went to Republicans. These newly identified players included the CEOs of oil companies: Smith International, Chevron, Texaco, Shell Oil, Ashland and Anadarko Petroleum. Also, on this list are powerful lobbyists including former Republican National Committee (RNC) chairman Haley Barbour. The Secretary also met with the Business Roundtable, an association of corporate executives who spent almost 9.7 million dollars on lobbying efforts in 2001 alone.

Needless to say the Bush energy plan relies heavily on fossil fuels and increased energy production and ignores, for the most part, both conservation and the development of alternative energy sources such as solar or wind power that would have a far more benign impact on the global environment. No representatives of labor, energy conservation and environmental groups or ordinary people were invited to offer their input into these meetings even though the public at large will ultimately have to pay dearly once these policies are fully implemented.

If the policies generated from closed door sessions are enacted, the environmental costs will be significant. The modern corporation makes decisions not based on the public good, but rather on the continual growth of profit and wealth. Corporate goals are essentially short term goals, and ultimately injurious to the planet's ability to sustain the biological diversity and complexity that is so crucial to human survival. The U.S. brand of capitalism is based on crazed thinking that is unmindful of the long term consequences of unabated energy-intensive economic progress.

Public policy is being crafted with the help and encouragement of the vested interests of the powerful leaving little room for dialog and discussion by the society at large. This model is essentially autocratic and does not deviate greatly from the idea of government that was originally envisioned by Alexander Hamilton.

The fact that public discourse has been stifled and so effectively circumvented has led to a feeling of powerlessness among the electorate. This, in turn, has resulted in an extreme apathy among those with no real access to government. Presently, any candidate who successfully wins an election does not represent a majority of the people, but at best less than 30 percent, since national elections tend to attract about 50 percent of all eligible voters. This is hardly a consensus. This obvious fact does not stop the media from representing electoral victories as proof of a consensus, for it is in their interest to do so.

In order for elections to gain the participation required to make them meaningful, voters must feel that they have real choices among candidates for office: candidates that do not require funding by the powerful in order to sustain their viability. Real campaign finance reform must be enacted as well as the public funding of campaigns and free access to the airways so that money is no longer the major consideration for candidacy. This would allow the interests of those other than the advantaged to be adequately represented. This idea, of course, has had an uphill battle made even more precarious by the participation of the national media in an inherently corrupt system. One of the more absurd arguments in defense of the present system is that any reform of the ways by which campaigns are financed would represent an infringement of the first amendment right of free speech. This suggests that wealthy contributors have a far greater right to free speech than small contributors and that, by inference, supporters of candidates who are unable to make any monetary contribution apparently have no free speech rights at all.

How else is democracy exercised? The simple fact of voting does not make for a democracy. Democracy should be a living and dynamic institution where the voice of the people is constantly heard, listened to and ultimately incorporated into public policy. This goal can be achieved provided there is the will to do so. Some of the necessary changes I envision are: the public financing of political campaigns, encouraging national discourse through a truly open and accessible government and supplying sufficient resources to social services so that the economically disadvantaged could have a greater opportunity to participate in the political life of the country. In other words, real change can be accelerated markedly by a commitment to an open society: a society that really honors the diverse and imaginative voice of the people. It is the furthering of all the people's interests that makes for true participatory democracy. What we have now radically diverges from that goal.

Over the years, various administrations in power have congratulated themselves on how instrumental they had been in spreading democracy throughout the world, especially in Latin America. One of the countries cited repeatedly as an example is Colombia, one of our closest allies in this regard. We will examine in some detail just how democratic this nation is.

Columbia is now in the midst of a civil war that the George W. Bush administration has re-defined as being a part of an international terrorist conspiracy. This perspective conveniently circumvents any discussion or analysis of the root causes of the civil war that is raging.

As of 2002, Columbia was considered to have the worst human rights record in Latin America. Civil war has been going on in Columbia since the 1940s. This war represents a conflict between the central government allied with wealthy landowners and a leftist insurgency. It has been a bloody conflict that has left over 35,000 dead in the past decade.

Seventeen million of the thirty-seven million Columbians live in poverty (46 percent) with about twelve million in extreme poverty (32 percent). A visiting representative of the Spanish government, Deputy Garcia, voiced the opinion that the "grave problems" he witnessed can be overcome with structural changes allowing for economic and social development and "a better distribution of wealth."

It has been estimated that since 1985 over 3,800 union workers and union leaders have been assassinated in Columbia. The unions in Columbia have been demanding a more equitable distribution of wealth. In this allegedly democratic country, the United States has committed billions of dollars in military aid to the Columbian government to help in its fight against the rebels, and in support of the ruling class as a way to further American economic interests. This is but one example of a long standing policy supported by a succession of administrations. This kind of alignment with the powerful represents the real political reality, and has little to do with supporting emerging democracies.

We are a nation that prides itself on the Bill of Rights. It has been shown repeatedly, however, that whenever such fundamental rights as free speech and free assembly threaten the power structure or the economic order, these rights are quickly and readily discarded as when Japanese American citizens were forcibly moved to detention camps during the Second World War and during the era of the so-called "Red Scare." This period of anti-communist hysteria is illustrative of how fear and demagoguery can be used effectively to silence people whose views are held to be dangerous.

That era of "McCarthyism," when serious constraints were placed on the basic freedoms of speech, expression and assembly, was preceded by the passage of the Alien Registration Act on June 29, 1940. This law made it a crime for any United States citizen to advocate, abet or teach the desirability of overthrowing the government. The law also mandated the registration of all alien residents over fourteen years of age. Registrants were also required to file a statement of their personal and occupational status as well as a record of their political beliefs. This law is remarkably analogous to the current Patriot Act as detailed in the Introduction of this book.

The fear of the American Communist Party and other left-leaning organizations inspired the creation of this law. It should be remembered that Communism was seen, since its inception, as a fundamental threat to capitalism. The vehicle for monitoring the activity of suspect groups was the House of Un-American Activities Committee that was established under Martin Dies in 1938 for the purpose of monitoring and investigating unpatriotic behavior.

In 1947, the House of Un-American Activities Committee began an investigation into the motion picture industry. The committee was chaired by J. Parnell Thomas. Those purported to have "left-wing" ideas were such notable figures as Bertolt Brecht. Ten of those brought before the committee refused to testify, citing the First Amendment. They were subsequently sent to prison. Those who continued to refuse to cooperate were blacklisted from the industry and prevented from finding work. There were 320 individuals that were placed on this list. They included: Leonard Bernstein, John Garfield, Howard Da Silva, Dashell Hammett, Lillian Hellman, Burl Ives, Arthur Miller, Dorothy Parker, Philip Loeb, Pete Seeger and Orson Welles.

Ultimately, the Alien Registration Act was used to pursue, harass and disrupt the American Communist Party. From October 1949, forty-six members of the party were arrested and accused of attempting to overthrow the government. In 1950, Senator Joseph McCarthy from Wisconsin claimed that communists had infiltrated the government. He established his political reputation on these claims. In reality, J. Edgar Hoover, Director of the FBI, was feeding information to McCarthy. All these machinations lead to a contagious anti-Communist hysteria throughout the country. It was not long before books that expressed views unfriendly to the government became targets. Many of these books were ultimately removed from the libraries. As McCarthy became more and more extreme, he began to make important enemies and was eventually discredited.

These actions need to be seen in the broader context of what was going on in the world. At that time, the Korean War was going badly, the Soviet Union had made significant advances in Eastern Europe and the Communists, under the leadership of Mao Tse Tung, had successfully overthrown the Chinese government. Americans were definitely anxious and afraid and, therefore, susceptible to extreme policies and demagoguery. There are obvious parallels between the era of McCarthyism and the domestic political situation in which the George W. Bush administration has used the fear of terrorism, as exemplified by September 11, to seek popular approval of its interventionist foreign policy, while at the same time attempting to curtail domestic freedoms and push a highly conservative domestic agenda.

Democracy, often spoken but not truly practiced, has become a hollow word mostly devoid of meaning. A truly democratic society should be a vital and dynamic expression of the popular will. The political climate in the United States is one in which the rule of law, the laws themselves and the kind and context of social relationships is determined by those who wield immense wealth and power. The concept of a government by and for the people has become an idea without true meaning or validity.

Freedom is another word that is used so often to define ourselves as a people. We seem to pride ourselves on this characteristic and base so many of our national celebrations on its cherished existence. We also use it as a measuring stick in proclaiming ourselves as morally superior to most other peoples on the earth.

Freedom is a word that has become a national password, used, over and over again, to bolster national pride. It is interesting to note that this belief has existed since the nation's inception in spite of the fact that the Native Americans, who survived the savage and brutal attempt at annihilation, were forced to live on reservations that comprised land that was considered worthless at the time. This belief was strongly held while the nation was actively importing and exploiting African slaves and treating them as property. America engaged in two world wars supposedly in defense of this freedom, while a significant portion of its population was denied equal access to education, employment, health care, housing and general individual advancement, based solely on the color of their skin. The United States, so enveloped in freedom, has one of the highest per capita prison populations (currently over two million individuals incarcerated) in the world, where a majority of those imprisoned are people of color, and public health statistics that are abysmal by international standards, with an egregious share of the national wealth in the hands of a very few. The actual extent of this inequity in the distribution of wealth will be examined in greater detail in Chapter Four of this book. Although some of the more terrible assaults on human civil rights have been corrected, a significant portion of the population is not as free as those who so glorify the virtues of this society. It seems that the reality of living in America does not fit well with the shared belief in the existence of a free society,

Freedom is not merely a theoretical construct. It is a living reality defined by its practice. I maintain that economic and political conditions are essentially inseparable and intertwined. In his seminal work entitled, *Development as Freedom*, Amartya Sen claims that "enhancement of human freedom is both the main object and the primary means of development." In his view freedom encompasses economic facilities, political freedoms, social opportunities, transparency guarantees and protective security. Freedom is not simply a political attribute, but has very practical manifestations such as accessibility to adequate health care, housing, etc.

It is the powerful that have the time and resources to exercise and experience freedom: the capacity to act from one's own will rather than be subjected to the will of others. The working class has no such luxury. A good portion of each day in the life of workers and their families is spent at the beck and call of employers who control and dominate their lives during the period of employment. Even under the protective umbrella of unions, workers are anything but free at the workplace. In fact, the profits made by employers, at the expense of workers, are used to insure that members of the ruling class can exercise their freedom without any real constraints. They can erect sprawling private estates, magnificent fortresses of wealth and power where their will is supreme. They employ servants to do all the menial chores that are a necessary part of modern existence. They can, on account of their wealth, exercise a degree of control over their own lives that makes them seemingly free agents.

The power of the employer over his/her workers is growing and extending beyond the confines of the workplace. Employees in many companies are expected to undergo lie detector tests and drug tests as a condition of employment. The rationale for these invasive practices is to prevent so-called drug abusers from gaining employment. This may be true, in part, but these practices also place more power in the hands of those who control production. Many workers have, in fact, become wage slaves living at the whim and caprice of their employers. Most employers attempt to increase profitability by controlling labor costs. This they do in a number of ways. They reduce the workforce shifting the burden of production to a smaller number of people. They either deny medical insurance benefits to their employees or insist on workers taking on a greater and greater share of the costs. They actively try to discourage unionization at the workplace. This insures that individual workers will have no access to the power of numbers that unions afford, when employees attempt to redress grievances. They decrease the size of the labor force by laying off workers when there is a decrease in demand for their products. The ultimate weapon that employers have is to relocate manufacturing abroad where pay and working conditions are abysmal. All these practices have led to a gradual decline in real wages, a permanent loss of manufacturing jobs and a shift to a service economy.

These same employers make substantial contributions to members of the legislature from both parties so as to guarantee that the government will not interfere with their agendas. If the sole purpose of corporations is profitability with no real sense of social responsibility, then the entire social fabric is held at risk.

There can no true freedom without economic freedom; there can be no true democracy without democracy at the workplace. It should be no surprise that corporate power has used all the formidable resources at its disposal, especially that of the media, to discredit the labor movement. There is power in numbers, and it will take great effort to mobilize public opinion and ultimately transform public policy. Organized labor has long been a powerful opponent of the exploitation of labor by capital. It is, indeed, tragic that working people have allowed themselves to accept this repudiation of unions to their own detriment. Without organized labor, wages have been suppressed, benefits have eroded and workloads and time on the job have increased markedly. It is now an economic reality that both parents must work to adequately support their family.

It is time for working people to come together and insist on and develop the democratic institutions that will give them a meaningful voice in determining what is produced and the means required to produce them. Organizing labor is a Herculean task. It requires determination, dedication and monumental effort. It will need to start modestly and build upon both success and failure.

There is a thirst among people for establishing a truly democratic society where freedom is no longer just a word used to justify all manner of detrimental behavior on the part of government and the powerful they so meaningfully represent. There is a hunger among people for a society where freedom is not just a commodity purchased by the powerful and denied everyone else. It is possible to fashion a world where more value is placed on the aspects of the heart and the mind than on the accumulation of material wealth and power.

Slavery is still very much with us though in a different guise. Debilitating economic structures must be seen for what they are and what they do to people. These structures that protect and defend wealth and perpetuate dynasties of the powerful must be reformed for justice to be made real. These are perilous times in which demagoguery has been given a very large voice. These are dangerous times in which truth is avoided at all cost, and the nation is wrapped up in delusions of its own invention. The government, through the voice of the corporate media, has painted a spurious picture of a surreal world in which we are engaged in a life and death struggle with evil and where we are the undeniable proponents of good. This Orwellian distortion of the truth flies in the face of history itself: a point that will be discussed in Chapter Three of this book. When societies reach this state of hysteria and unreason, terrible things are bound to happen. All manner of brutality and butchery can be lauded and condoned, for once we have made the enemy a devil, behavior knows no bounds and deplorable acts become possible. This is what we risk as a people and a nation when we rebuke reason and accrue all power to ourselves. It is the way so many empires have declined and fallen in the past, and it is a pattern that seems bound to repeat itself.

2

The Myth of Equal Justice

There is a current myth that has been promulgated by politicians, with the indispensable help of the media, that we have somehow become a color blind society in which all persons are treated equally and with equal justice for all. According to this myth, the goal of equality of opportunity that the civil rights movement has been involved with for so long, and with so much passion, has been successfully achieved. This rationale has been used effectively to roll back the gains made through affirmative action programs in many states, including California and Washington.

The degree to which white Americans agree with an assessment that flies in the face of reality belies the extent to which racism is woven into the fabric of our culture. Black males continue to fill the nation's prisons in record numbers, far in excess of their representation in the general population. There are currently over two million prisoners in the United States, one of the highest per capita rates in the world. This translates to approximately one out of every 150 people in the United States living in jail.

From averages taken from twenty-nine states and the District of Columbia where these data have been released, African American males make up 48 percent of the total prison population though they are 11.6 percent of the total population, whereas non-Hispanic whites make up 38.7 percent of the prison population where they represent 74.8 percent of the total population. These data are represented graphically below (Chart 1).

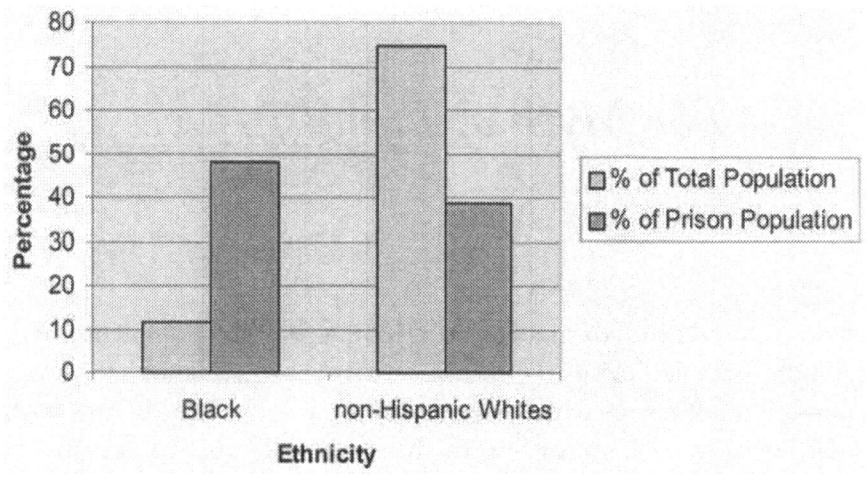

Chart 1 Percentage of Prison Inmates Based on Ethnicity and Compared to their Representation in the Entire Population

In addition, non-Hispanic blacks were 42.3 percent of all local jail inmates in June 2000 whereas non-Hispanic whites were 41.9 percent of jail inmates in 2000. Most cities have black ghettoes that are invariably plagued by poverty and unemployment. Crime is strongly associated with economic conditions, and poor black and Hispanic areas are the primary focus of police action. African Americans are less likely to have adequate health care, suffer from high infant mortality rates and their children, more often than not, attend inferior schools. These statistics do not lend much credence to the idea of a color blind society. Quite to the contrary, the nation is bounded by racism. It is a direct result of the legacy of slavery, an abominable practice that the nation, to this day, fails to address. There can be no true justice for black citizens and people of color while racism, and the attitudes that it engenders, continues to play such a significant role in the wider culture.

This inequality of treatment before the law between blacks and whites is also mirrored in the disparity of treatment between the classes. Put in its simplest terms, a poor man in California can be given life imprisonment for the shoplifting of videotapes due to the State's "three strikes and you're out" law, while an executive from the Enron corporation who has stolen millions from his employees' pension funds as well as the millions upon millions from the energy ratepayers of California has yet to serve any jail time. One might ask how this is possible. To answer this question, one must ask who creates and frames the laws and to whom are they held accountable. Laws designed to protect wealth are ironclad, and the victims of these laws are invariably the powerless, i.e. the poor. The poor person accused of a crime has very limited access to competent counsel, and must depend upon a public defender, poorly paid, and often entirely unmotivated. Those who break such laws find themselves in prison for long stretches of time. On the other hand, laws designed to hold the wealthy accountable are filled with ambiguities and loopholes that any competent attorney can use to effectively spare his or her client the discomfort and inconvenience of jail time.

These are not simply anecdotal examples. Not many wealthy individuals are likely to be found in the nation's jails. If they happen to go through the entire process of indictment, trial, conviction and sentencing, they most probably will be sent to low security prisons. The system of justice is skewed in their favor. It is the height of hypocrisy to suggest otherwise.

It is the poor, regardless of race, that populate the nation's prisons. The number of Americans behind bars increased by more than 76,000 in 2001. About two hundred new prison cells are constructed in the United States every day at a cost of about 10 million dollars a day, while spending for higher education has been cut by about 18 percent. A cut in the funding for higher education increases the likelihood of crime in those areas where a good education is most desperately needed. Laws are often crafted to protect the wealthy, and it is law enforcement agencies that are required to enforce those laws. The police often find themselves caught between these two warring classes.

The myth of equal justice is effectively portrayed by the television media, time and time again, with a plethora of "cop shows" which show the police as diligent public servants that protect society from the lawless. The criminals in these televised dramas are depicted as deranged or sinister and always evil. The police and the justice system are shown as the purveyors of good and keepers of justice: there to capture and incarcerate wrong doers for the public good. What they fail to show is the daily harassment, surveillance, detention and prosecution that are disproportionately visited on the people of poor neighborhoods in the inner core of many American cities. These areas have a majority of non-white individuals, who live under the onus of a grinding poverty with inadequate housing, health and child care and inferior education. They are somehow expected to live within the norms established by the more affluent members of society. The role of law enforcement in these areas is containment. The punishment is accordingly harsh to accomplish this goal. Why is it that the punishment for the use and sale of crack cocaine is so much higher than for the use and sale of the cocaine powder, which is, after all, the drug of choice of the affluent? Why is it that such harsh sentences are meted out for crimes such as shoplifting and many other non-violent offenses? The message is a clear one: business, corporate interests and the security and safety of the well-to-do must be protected at all costs. There are only but a few avenues for the poor to rise above their poverty. All "illicit" methods are actively discouraged.

There can be no true justice and equality of treatment before the law without economic justice and equality. If all members of society were viewed as valued and treated accordingly, they would have equal access to good quality housing, education and health care, and equal justice before the law would follow. If labor was viewed as a respected and essential part of the national economy, and not just as a commodity to be exploited, the minimum wage would be a living wage. If the security and well being of all Americans were truly a goal of the culture at large, there would be no one, especially children, going hungry, there would be no homeless, there would be no one living in abject poverty, and no child would be subjected to an abysmally inferior education.

Economic justice appears to be incompatible with the American brand of capitalism. Within the current system, everything is valued only in so much as profit can be made. Health care has been commandeered by the pharmaceutical and insurance companies. There is a move to privatize public education, and even the prison system is being infiltrated by private for profit companies. Although the tobacco companies that have been selling a lethal product for many years are now subject to domestic scrutiny, no one has questioned their right to export this product overseas for the purpose of profit, with the ultimate cost of millions upon millions of lives. Within such an infrastructure, the needs of people that do not engender the possibility of profit are disregarded and neglected. Within such a system, gross inequities become possible and inevitable. In this environment, a two tier system has emerged where a very small percentage of the population controls an overwhelming portion of the wealth and, therefore, power and influence, leaving everyone else struggling for the leftovers.

The organization of American society is one in which leadership comes from the top, from those few with wealth and power, and where the mass of humanity finds itself conforming to a way of living designed to accommodate the agenda of the powerful. This structure has never really worked and has been shown to be critically flawed and corrupt. The very survival of the species and the viability of the planet are at risk. A way out of this quagmire is a restructuring of the social order so that power and wealth are more equitably distributed and where people have a more meaningful and direct control of their own destinies.

The way to transform this system is not by violent insurrection led by an elitist group or faction, for, as history has demonstrated so often in the past, this will only lead to replacing one powerful minority with another. The most viable method is one accomplished by a peaceful transition brought about by a truly mass movement demanding change. There are many groups that are currently active in promoting structural change, but they are scattered and, therefore, ineffective. The needs are many: adequate housing, medical care, prison reform, education, child care, meaningful work and a living wage. These are goals that are attainable through a merging and coalescence of these activist groups and their energies.

A major obstacle to the coming together of these disparate voices is government and corporate propaganda, which enlists the reach and effectiveness of the private media. These forces must be countered with a persistent and wide ranging program designed to educate people to the realities of this system and to propose and invite solutions from all sectors of the population. It is a non-violent struggle that must be waged from many fronts, a battle fought for particular and reachable goals such as food for the hungry, housing for the homeless, health care for those without, etc. Small victories and many of them will maintain the momentum for change, and lead, in my view, to larger and more unexpected gains. The fundamental goal of these efforts should be the improvement of the human condition and the ultimate achievement of universal equal justice.

3

Foreign Policy and the Myth of the World Policeman

Many Americans still hold onto the idea that America serves as a kind of world policeman keeping the world and its people safe and free. This is a remarkable notion, given the weight of historical evidence that paints an entirely different picture. Individuals most susceptible to this kind of propaganda are those poorly read and those who need to feel that their country is a good nation maintaining itself in a hostile world filled with nations and peoples with hateful ideas and evil motives. Governments, in general, play on this need, and constantly portray themselves as being on the side of good battling the forces of evil. This self image becomes grossly exaggerated during dangerous times, especially that of war.

President, George W. Bush, and his administration has referred to our national enemies as evil. The candidates he chose for this role are the countries of Iraq, Iran and North Korea. It is important to note that these countries are third world countries incapable of defending themselves against the formidable power of the United States military. They were collectively accused of being a part of the "axis of evil" and of perpetrating horrendous crimes against humanity and harboring weapons of mass destruction. This self righteous posturing is coming from a country that has the most deadly and pervasive arsenal of weapons of mass destruction on the entire planet, and has repeatedly used these weapons to further and protect whatever is deemed to be in the national (i.e. economic) interest. One must, therefore, conclude that we harbor such weapons for the good, and those who are our enemy have only bad intentions. This, itself, is a remarkable idea, since the United States is also the only country in history that has used nuclear weapons against civilian populations. It certainly seems to be mysterious, if not self-serving logic. We are living in a time when double speak seems to be the norm. Surprisingly, there are very few voices that question these assertions and proclamations.

Let us examine this notion of our good and noble intentions in the world in juxtaposition with historic reality. We will begin with World War II. I have decided to begin at this point in history, because this war represented the turning point that catapulted the United States into the role of a super power. The Second World War has been viewed for these past sixty years as a kind of Holy Grail. Supposedly, we saved the world from the insidious and voracious jaws of Fascism. Of course, the horrendous atrocities perpetrated by Germany and Japan cannot be denied or underestimated. The world view embodied by Fascism was so extreme that it invited retaliation. The slaughter of millions of innocent human beings, including six million Jews, to achieve crazed and fanatical goals was totally unacceptable and had to be opposed. But does that provide a carte blanche in terms of retaliation? I believe that we need to examine our behavior in that conflict. This analysis should include an examination of the carnage and human suffering brought upon civilians in the fire bombing of German and Japanese cities and the use of atomic weapons against Hiroshima and Nagasaki.

The allies decided upon a policy of bombing entire cities and towns, a tactic which the Germans regarded as "terror bombing." One strategy used was the creation of firestorms. Firestorms occurred as the result of dropping incendiary bombs containing highly combustible magnesium, phosphorus or petroleum jelly commonly referred to as napalm. These devices were dropped in clusters. Once an area caught fire, the temperatures were so high that the hot air rose rapidly causing cold air to rush in at ground level. This effect literally sucked people into the fire. In 1945, the target chosen for this strategy was the German city of Dresden. The population of the city at that time was well over 650,000 due to large numbers of people fleeing from the advancing Red Army. On February 13, 1945 the attack began. Dresden was almost completely annihilated. Estimates of the number of German civilians killed range from 135,000 to 250,000 thousand, a number far exceeding the 51,509 British citizens killed at the hands of the German Lufwaffe during the entire war. The dead bodies stacked like cordwood, most burned beyond recognition, were reminiscent of the bodies of the Jews found at the German concentration camps.

To give a further idea of the scale of destruction, of the 28,410 houses in the inner city, 24,866 were destroyed. Many of those in air raid shelters died as a result of lack of oxygen consumed by the immense fires above ground. The heat was so intense that many thousands were completely incinerated. In addition, the morning after, American fighter planes fired directly into crowds of refugees fleeing from the holocaust.

By any measure these acts were crimes against humanity, but the Nuremberg trials were not intended to try the victors, only the vanquished. This is but one example of the war of terror waged against civilian populations that make the German blitz against the city of London seem miniscule in comparison.

An excellent demonstration of the extent to which American culture is in denial regarding its own actions are the events that transpired when the Enola Gay, the plane that carried one of the atomic bombs dropped on Japanese cities, was placed in the Smithsonian Air and Space Museum in Washington DC. In the summer of 1993, the museum began planning a show about the atomic bombing of Japanese cities and the end of World War II that was to accompany the display of the hull of the Enola Gay. Several veteran organizations expressed concern over the nature of the show. After many script revisions, the display was dramatically reduced to a plaque and a video about the crew. In a statement by Michael Heyman, Secretary of the Smithsonian Institution, in an attempt to explain this decision, he said, "This morning I shared with the Board of Regents my decision to replace "The Last Act: The Atomic Bomb and the End of World War II" scheduled to open in May at the National Air and Space Museum. I have taken this action for one overriding reason: I have concluded that we made a basic error in attempting to couple an historical treatment of the use of atomic weapons with the 50th anniversary commemoration of the end of the war. Exhibitions have many purposes, equally worthwhile. But we need to know which of the many goals is paramount, and not to confuse them."

We do not want any reminders of our own culpability. We want to be able to honor the Enola Gay and its crew without having to reflect on what was actually done. The extent of the suffering of the residents of Hiroshima and Nagasaki as the result of the nuclear bombs exploded over their cities has, of course, been documented in exquisite detail. In addition to the thousands incinerated instantaneously (perhaps the lucky ones), thousands upon thousands of men, women and children suffered unimaginable pain from radiation burns and an agonizingly slow death as a result of the destruction of the bone marrow not to mention the genetic damage that resulted from exposure to massive doses of radiation that has effected their descendents to this day. By year's end (1945), 140,000 residents of Hiroshima died as a direct result of the attack. These unfortunate people endured a living hell. A stirring first hand account about what transpired can be found in the novels entitled, *Black Rain* by Masuji Ibuse and *Hiroshima* by John Hersey. Are not the perpetrators of this attack guilty of crimes against humanity using exactly the same standards that are used by the American leadership when it comes to accusations made against the governments of the so-called "rogue states"?

So much of what is considered patriotic is the idolatry of our fabulous weapons of war, yet no connection is made between these weapons and what they are designed to do. No acknowledgement is ever made regarding the relationship between the instruments of war and their obvious effects. World War II is often used as an example of a "just war." Can a war be just if it's filled with unjust acts leading to untold misery and death?

It is clear that the harsh conditions imposed by the Treaty of Versailles contributed significantly to the perverse social and economic conditions in pre-war Germany that made the population susceptible to the crazed agenda of Adolph Hitler. We are not encouraged to seriously examine why the Japanese launched an attack on Pearl Harbor. Was it as unprovoked as it seemed? Was it simply a nefarious and wholly unjustified act perpetrated by an evil and aggressive nation?

The London Naval Treaty of 1930 involving Japan, Great Britain and the United States required that Japan make no attempt to maintain its supremacy over the American fleet in their own home waters, and compromised Japan's own plans for regional control. Japanese domestic opposition to this treaty was intense. In general, the Japanese felt that the Western countries were unfair in demanding a status quo, in which Western powers retained supremacy. The Japanese pursued policies to ensure their own regional hegemony, and felt that they were being stymied by the Western powers. They felt pressure from the expansionist powers of China and the Soviet Union that were establishing a presence on the Manchurian border. The feeling that the government had capitulated to Western interests provided an impetus to a growing fascist movement. The schism between the policies of the civilian Japanese government, which tended to play according to Western rules, and the nationalistic Kwantung Army had grown wider and wider.

The depression of 1929 had hit hard in Japan. By 1931, America had supplanted Japan as the major exporter to China, and Japanese exports to the United States decreased dramatically in part as a result of the Smoot-Hawley tariff of 1930. By 1932, Japan had successfully engineered the creation of the independent state of Manchuria which they controlled through a local Chinese government loyal to Japanese interests, and had dispatched troops to Shanghai. This strategy is analogous to the U.S. government's activities in Vietnam following the defeat of the French colonialists. The League of Nations had sent a commission of inquiry, the Lytton Commission, to look into the Manchurian situation. The commission's findings rejected the Japanese position that Manchukuo be established as an independent sovereignty. Rather than capitulate, Japan withdrew from the League of Nations. Events would soon cycle out of control and lead to a terrible war that plunged the world into darkness.

The argument that governments are sometimes called upon to resort to war to oppose an "aggressor" nation is refuted by the renowned pacifist A.J. Muste who, in his book entitled, *Non-violence in an Aggressive World* (1940), claimed that "The line-up in the world is read in terms of "peace-loving" versus "persistently aggressive" nations. That is superficial and misleading. It is the same reading that brought us disaster twenty years ago. The real line-up is between satiated powers, determined to hang on to the 85 percent of the earth's vital resources which they control, even if that means plunging the world into another war, and another set of powers equally determined to change the imperialist status even it that means plunging the world into another war." In my mind this is a very prophetic argument. He goes on to caution that as soon as a nation finds itself on the path of war preparation, it strengthens the forces on the right and moves the society towards fascism. This observation is certainly supported by the current climate in the United States with the enactment of the Patriot Act and the beginnings of the increasing curtailment of individual civil liberties. The proposal by the extremist Attorney General John Ashroft that Americans should spy on each other under the guise of national security, demonstrates the extent to which fear has been used as a tool to control the population.

In regards to war preparations prior to World War II, A. J. Muste further states, "The United States is not ready for disarmament and war-renunciation. What then shall we propose? A little war-preparation, purely defensive preparation, refined economic warfare which can be safely waged at a distance against supposedly sinful nations? Surely they are no alternatives at all (such as moderate war-preparations in this day!), or they are alternatives which lead straight to disaster." History has demonstrated again and again that war is no solution. It simply leads the future into the ineluctable direction of further conflict and suffering.

The political establishment decries any attempt to question President Truman's motivations for authorizing the use of nuclear weapons against Japan at a time when the Japanese were preparing to sue for peace. Truman made the following entry into his diary on July 25, 1945, "…This weapon is to be used against Japan between now and August 10th. I have told the Sec. of War, Mr. Stimpson, to use it so that military objectives and soldiers and sailors are the target and not women and children. Even if the Japs are savages, ruthless, merciless and fanatic, we as the leader of the world for the common welfare cannot drop that terrible bomb on the old capital or the new." In spite of this entry, the President approved the order to use the bomb, "on one of the targets: Hiroshima, Kokura, Niigata and Nagasaki." In his book entitled, *The Politics of War: The World and United States Foreign Policy 1943-1945*, Gabriel Kolko maintains that the real purpose behind the decision to use nuclear weapons against the Japanese people was to, "create terror among the Soviets." The Soviet Union at that time was preparing to enter the Pacific theatre.

How many innocent civilians died at our hands by the end of that war? Is it possible that the number far exceeded the six million casualties of the holocaust? I maintain that these are questions that should be asked if we, as a species, are ever to end the cycle of devastation and destruction that comes with the rise and fall of empires that have plagued human civilization from its beginnings.

Before the war's end, the leaders of Great Britain, the United States and the then Soviet Union met on the Crimean Sea at the Yalta Conference. Winston Churchill, Franklin Roosevelt and Josef Stalin met and drafted secret agreements that in effect were plans to establish spheres of political and economic interest after the war was won. The victors planned to divide up the spoils of war, taking full advantage of the chaos that was looming over the ravaged planet. Such is the nature of war and its aftermath.

The world is changing: cultural barriers between peoples are eroding rapidly. The revolution in communications is bringing diverse peoples together. Americans can either resist this change by building a fortress around themselves or choose to join the family of nations. It is imperative that we begin to see our nation and its past as belonging to the fabric of human history, with all is flaws and imperfections, and not as requiring a special exalted space in it. Maintaining a delusional self-image of superiority is inimical to further development.

The story of war, unfortunately, does not end with the Second World War. Many wars have followed, both large and small. They need to be enumerated: the Korean War, the Vietnam War, the proxy wars against Chile, Nicaragua, Guatemala, Cuba, El Salvador, and wars against Panama, Granada, Afghanistan and Iraq. These do not include the use of weapons of mass destruction against Cambodia, Laos, Libya, Somalia and Sudan. It is interesting to note that all these countries are poor and underdeveloped with one exception, Iraq. Iraq, a nation with a significant and prospering middle class, was made terribly poor and backward as a result of both war and the subsequent economic sanctions that were imposed upon its people. Economic sanctions, in fact, have become a wholly new kind of insidious and deadly warfare and collective punishment, where innocents are the guaranteed victims, a kind of bloodless terror.

What were the provocations for all these conflicts? Was the nation's national security ever seriously in jeopardy in any of these military confrontations? These are the questions that need to be addressed.

The Korean War was never called a war but a United Nation's "police action" directed against the incursion of North Korea into the South. Although there was some representation by other nations, the United States played a predominant role in the conflict. The invasion of South Korea by the North Korean communists was seen as a dangerous act that threatened the spread of communism into the Asian theatre. It did not, however, represent an immediate threat to the security of the United States. The decision to intervene in Korea was essentially a political one emanating from a fear of the communist ideology. Furthermore, this situation was exacerbated by the decision by the United States to use its forces, under the leadership of General Macarthur, to push into the North, leading to the involvement of China in the conflict. The behavior of the United States in that conflict deserves some attention.

The conflagration went on for three years. In those years, the people of North Korea suffered grievously. As part of the overall war strategy, the dykes that supplied the water to the rice paddies in the North were bombed. In this case innocent farmers and the people who depended upon them for food were targeted. Five of North Korea's major cities were completely destroyed. The estimates of civilian casualties in North Korea range in the millions. It is estimated that 20 percent of the North Korean population were killed during the war. Former U.S. Air Force Chief of Staff Curtis LeMay stated, "We slipped a note...under the door into the Pentagon and said, "Look, let us go up there...and burn down five of the biggest towns in North Korea—and they're not very big—and that ought to stop it. Well the answer to this was four or five screams—'You'll kill a lot of noncombatants!—and 'It's too horrible!' Yet over a period of three years or so...we burned down every town in North Korea and South Korea too....Now, over a period of three years this is palatable, but to kill a few people to stop this from happening—a lot of people can't stomach it." This is a unique insight into the mentality of those who are left with the "business" of waging war.

This behavior again constitutes what can be regarded as war crimes or crimes against humanity. The powerful are never charged with such criminality, it is only the vanquished that suffer in this way. This is not to suggest that atrocities were not committed by the other side. Atrocities seem to be a "natural" outcome of war, a time when reason succumbs to chaos and depravity. The end result of all of this destruction was the maintenance of the status quo: the division of Korea into the North and South. It is important to know the details of such events so that we do not further delude ourselves as a nation regarding our own motivations and actions.

Much has been written about the Vietnam War. What is clear and unmistakable is that it began as a civil war between two conflicting political ideologies. The nationalist-communist group from the North, under the leadership of the immensely popular Ho Chi Minh, was in conflict with the right wing forces from the South supported by the West, especially the United States. There was never a North and South Vietnam. This was a contrivance of the West to further its own interests in the region. The United States, in fact, took over the colonial position after the French had left in disarray and defeat. Internal documents reveal American interests in tin and rubber and a concern about the potential loss of the bountiful resources of Indonesia should communism spread throughout the region. These economic interests were camouflaged by anti-communist rhetoric and propaganda advanced by the government and directed towards the American public as a rationale for its intervention. As a matter of fact, the so-called Gulf of Tonkin incident, in which it was claimed that Vietnamese enemy had launched an attack against U.S. ships in international waters, was later revealed to be a fabrication. This incident involved the U.S.S. Maddox, a naval destroyer. It was in international waters gathering intelligence information. It was allegedly attacked by North Vietnamese torpedo boats. Only two Senators, Wayne Morse and Ernest Gruening from Oregon and Alaska, respectively, voted against the resolution passed by the Senate, in August of 1964, granting the President the right to use whatever means deemed necessary to redress this supposed act of aggression.

Once the United States entered the conflict, many unspeakable atrocities were launched against the peoples of Vietnam including: use of anti-personnel weapons against civilian populations, use of napalm against villages and deforestation of one quarter of the countryside with the highly toxic Agent Orange. Human exposure to this chemical leads to birth defects, abortions and cancer still suffered by the Vietnamese people some forty years after the conflict. As of January 2003, the U.S. government has admitted a correlation between a certain kind of leukemia (CLL) and exposure of American soldiers to Agent Orange while in Vietnam. In response to this acknowledgment, the government plans to offer some kind of compensation to these unfortunate individuals. However, not one word has been spoken regarding the government's culpability in inflicting this disease on many Vietnamese civilians who had the misfortune to be living in the path of this deadly chemical. The fact that a society that proclaims its indefatigable morality to the whole world can ignore this magnitude of suffering caused by its own actions, speaks volumes regarding the level of apathy, indifference and a lack of moral conviction.

In addition to these atrocities, one can not exclude from consideration: the carpet bombing of Vietnamese cities especially Hanoi, the destruction of many villages, the mass displacement of whole populations and documented massacres of civilians. Some two million Vietnamese died as a result of this conflict. This does not include the illegal air war against Laos and Cambodia that destroyed the fragile infrastructure of these small defenseless countries, and set the stage for the chaos that followed. Laotian children to this day are being maimed and killed by inadvertently triggering land mines left by the United States. The U.S. government has steadfastly refused to release the specifications for these mines that would help aid organizations dismantle them, under the guise of protecting military secrets.

The American public eventually became disillusioned with this conflict, especially after so many young American lives were lost (over 59,000). It is hard to say just how long the conflict would have continued if American casualties were small in number. Currently, all manner of memorials have been built to commemorate the American dead. This is fitting, since those who lost their lives, as in all modern wars, were essentially from the poor and lower middle classes without the requisite assets and influence to avoid being drafted. They were as much victims as were the millions of Vietnamese. They were the pawns in a savage game of power. How many memorials have been built to honor the Vietnamese dead? How much recognition has been given to those Vietnamese still suffering from cancer, birth defects and premature death brought on by the poisons we have sown into their soil? The answer to these questions is appallingly obvious. America, as a nation, is in denial regarding its own brutal and reckless behavior. The blood of innocent victims has flown dark and red in great volumes both here and around the world for no other purpose than to serve the insatiable interests of the powerful.

The United States has never taken any responsibility for these criminal acts. As a matter of fact, it has now become popular for some historical revisionists to claim that the United States did not err in its excesses, but was actually too cautious and should have completed the destruction it began. In that way it would have been victorious. Is this the behavior of a benign nation that only acts to secure the peace and security of freedom loving peoples around the world? Not one cent has gone to reparations for the peoples of Vietnam. Is this the hallmark of a great, noble and just Christian nation? Let the deeds speak for themselves.

What were the lessons learned from this conflict? The military learned that there is vulnerability in keeping the public informed about its business and allowing too many American soldiers to become casualties. Therefore, a tighter leash has been maintained around the press, and more dependence has been placed on so-called "smart weapons" and robot killing devices that can wreck untold destruction without the risk of losing American lives. This change in policy was demonstrated in future conflicts, the best example being that of the war against Iraq to be examined in detail later in this chapter.

In the midst of the Vietnam War, there were events unfolding in Indonesia that have since been linked with the involvement of the United States government. What transpired can not be considered anything but a bloodbath. Between October 1, 1965 and April or May of the following year, the right-wing Generals Nasution and Suharto took full control of the government and, in a matter of months, as many as one million Indonesians were murdered. The murders were on such a scale that corpses filled the rivers in many parts of the country. The press in the United States and the Congress were strangely quiet while this was going on.

Indonesia was under colonial rule of the Dutch for about 350 years, and was occupied by the British for a brief period of time. During this prolonged era of exploitation, many of Indonesia's bountiful resources were plundered, while the Indonesian people remained terribly poor. It was not until after World War II that a growing nationalist movement had successfully risen up against the colonialists and displaced them.

The U.S. had become economically involved in Indonesia, referred to as Netherlands East Indies at the time, in the early 1900s. At that time, Standard Oil Company attempted to disrupt the monopoly of Indonesian oil maintained by the Dutch. Ultimately, Standard Oil began drilling for oil in Java in 1914. The U.S. also moved into rubber production while World War I was raging in Europe. Goodyear Tire and Rubber owned the largest rubber estates in the world. It should be kept in mind that Indonesia ranks fifth in the world in the extent of richness of its natural resources. Southeast Asia emerged as a primary focus in Washington's global strategy. The possible "loss" of Indonesia to the communists was, therefore, of great concern to the policy makers in the United States. It was deemed so important that that United States was financing some 80 percent of the French war effort before its defeat at Dien Bien Phu. In 1953, Eisenhower addressed the Governor's Conference. There he stated that it was essential that U.S. pay for the French war, for it was the riches of Indonesia that was at the heart of the matter.

In Arthur Schlesinger's *A Thousand Days*, his biography of President Kennedy, he relates the fact that Kennedy saw Indonesia, rich in oil, tin and rubber, as a significant nation of Asia and was concerned about its movement towards the Communist bloc.

Before the tragedy that befell this country, Indonesia had the largest communist party outside of the so-called socialist countries. The party was strong, vibrant and growing, much to the consternation of the American government. The Indonesian government, under the leadership of Sukarno, had expropriated British and American holdings and had turned down American economic aid.

The September 30th movement assassinated six right-wing Indonesian generals, but was subdued quickly on the morning of October 1, 1965. This event was viewed by the American press as an attempted coup although it probably was not the case. It seems that on September 21 of that year, there was a secret meeting of the Council of Generals headed by Nasution and Suharto. At this meeting, plans were drawn up to overthrow the government on October 5. The CIA was most likely involved in this plot. The historic record clearly shows that the CIA was involved in an unsuccessful coup attempt in 1958. When Sukarno learned of the most recent plot, the September 30th Movement was hastily formed. To further support the claim of American involvement, the U.S. was financing the Council of Generals with some 60 million dollars by 1963, equipped 43 battalions of the army and trained 200 high ranking officers. In fact, the United States continued to fund this organization of right-wing generals after President Sukarno had already rejected American aid. The U.S. government was determined to replace the government of Sukarno with a friendlier regime regardless of the cost to the Indonesian people. These efforts ultimately paid off.

It is informative to understand what happened to American investments immediately following the installation of this right-wing government. Companies such as Unilever, Uniroyal, Union Carbide, Singer Sewing Machine and National Cash Register quickly got back their expropriated properties. Mobil Oil secured oil exploration rights in Sumatra, and Freeport Sulphur got a $75 million contract for exploiting copper. U.S. steel had its sights on nickel and cobalt.

The government of President Sukarno was viewed as an impediment to the expansion of American economic interests. The wealth of natural resources in Indonesia was seen as far more important than the well being of the Indonesian people. This is the way that imperialist powers classically operate. It is a reality one can barely argue against given the events as they transpired. The media, however, made no real attempt to report these events as they were occurring, for it would expose an integral component of American foreign policy. The United States would once again support the murderous behavior of right-wing elements in Indonesia in regards to East Timor, as will be discussed later in this chapter.

After the Vietnamese conflict, the United States was still fully engaged in military interventions, but not as overtly as before. It functioned more secretly through its clients throughout the world. This was particularly evident in its policies towards the countries of Central and South America. The government, under both Republican and Democratic administrations, was busy funding and financing brutal regimes in Guatemala, Nicaragua, Honduras, El Salvador, Chile, Columbia, etc. Policies were in place to prop up authoritarian governments that supported U.S. economic hegemony throughout the region through outright economic and, more importantly, military aid. It was busy subverting democracy in Chile ultimately toppling (with the assistance of the CIA) the democratically elected government of Salvador Allende, and paving the way for the brutal regime of Pinochet responsible for the "disappearance" of thousands of political opponents. In a now famous comment, Kissinger said, while referring to Chile, that he saw no reason why a certain country should be allowed to "go Marxist" merely because "its people are irresponsible." Dr. Salvador Allende's socialist agenda deeply concerned such corporate interests as ITT, Pepsi Cola and Chase Manhattan Bank. In a meeting with CIA director Richard Helms, Nixon made his intentions clear that, "Allende was not to assume office." The use of tactics of subversion and outright intervention in the affairs of another country to achieve political ends was by no means a novel strategy.

In 1954, the democratically elected government of Arbenz in Guatemala was likewise overthrown. On May 23, 1997, under pressure from the U.S. Congress and on account of the Freedom of Information Act, the CIA released 1400 pages of documents, of an estimated 100,000 pages, detailing its involvement in the overthrow of the democratically elected government of Jacobo Arbenz Guzman of Guatemala. They detail a strategy designed to impose upon a sovereign nation the will of the United States in order to further its own economic and political interests.

When Arbenz assumed the presidency in 1950, he began to carry out modest land reforms that were in opposition to the American owned United Fruit Company (UF). He, in fact, nationalized 500,000 acres "owned" by UF. In 1952, President Harry Truman authorized the shipping of guns and money to support and train mercenaries opposed to the Arbenz government.

These covert operations were continued and expanded after Dwight D. Eisenhower became President. Before assuming public life, John

Foster Dulles, the Secretary of State, was a lawyer for the UF, and his brother, Allen Dulles, became the CIA director.

The CIA-sponsored Guatemalan Destabilization Program was given the code word "PBSUCCESS." This operation was authorized by Eisenhower in August of 1953. The details of this program included a publication entitled, *A Study of Assassination* which was, in fact, a guide to assassination. The overall goal of the CIA was to use methods of psychological warfare, political action and subversion to ensure the overthrow of the Arbenz government.

The CIA worked in collaboration with the notorious president of Nicaragua, Anastasio Somoza. These revealing documents show that the CIA had recommended the elimination of 58 individuals it deemed dangerous in a so-called "disposal list." Since the names themselves were expunged from the public record, it is difficult to determine if these assassinations were ever successfully carried out.

On June 27, 1954, Arbenz fled the country and was replaced by General Castillo Armas, a friend to the United States. Over the following years, Guatemalan military leaders were responsible for the death and injury of tens of thousands of political opponents from the left.

Some thirty years later, during the Presidency of Ronald Reagan, an analogous scenario of intervention in the political and economic life of another nation took place, this time in neighboring Nicaragua. In 1936, Anastasio Samoza took over the Nicaraguan presidency and remained in control for 43 years. His regime was infamous in regards to the level of violence and corruption. The Nicaraguan National Guard, under his control, operated as a death squad eliminating Samoza's political opponents. During his reign, two thirds of the population made less than 300 dollars a year, while his estimated worth was over 900 million dollars.

On July 19, 1979, the revolutionary Sandinista Party overthrew the Samoza regime. Immediately, upon assuming power, the new government instituted policies that involved land reform, social justice and the redistribution of wealth and income. This change in the political landscape set off alarm bells within the Carter administration. It was not long before President Jimmy Carter signed a secret finding authorizing the CIA to provide political support to the opponents of the Sandinistas. This support included CIA sponsored propaganda and support of paramilitary bands that engaged in operations in the North of the country.

Once Ronald Reagan assumed the U.S. presidency, CIA involvement escalated. Included in the overall planning was the covert allocation of 14 million dollars to help the Argentinean dictatorship train guerilla forces operating in camps in Honduras. Former Nicaraguan Nation Guard members helped form the basis of these forces ultimately referred to as the Contras.

The Contras employed terror tactics to accomplish the primary goal of replacing the Sandinista government with one more closely affiliated with the right. They were responsible for attacks on Nicaraguan development projects, economic co-operatives, educational facilities, health services and attacks on the infrastructure including bridges, power plants, hospitals and schools. They also caused excessive damage to crop fields, grain silos, irrigation projects, farm houses and machinery.

The Witness for Peace organization and Americas Watch documented lists of Contra-related atrocities including rape, torture, maiming, and male and female castrations. It was this group that Reagan referred to as "freedom fighters," and the "moral equal of our founding fathers."

In spite of the actions taken by Congress to halt aid to the Contras, financial assistance continued through a covert money laundering scheme headed by Oliver North. A trade embargo was imposed in which Nicaraguan sugar imports were cut by 90%. The IMF and World Bank withheld granting loans to Nicaragua, and Exxon refused to supply tankers to ship oil from Mexico to Nicaragua. All these actions were designed to seriously impact the Nicaraguan economy and consequently create hardships for its people.

In 1984, the CIA was directly involved in mining Nicaragua's harbors; an action that the World Court ruled as illegal. As a direct result of U.S. sponsored Contra activity, over 150,000 people were displaced from their homes and communities. Bridges, port facilities, granaries, water and oil depots, power stations, telephone equipment, saw mills, health centers, schools and dams were either destroyed or damaged. In October of 1984, the House Intelligence Committee authorized the publication of a guerilla-warfare training manual entitled, *Psychological Operations in Guerilla warfare.* This manual gave advice regarding political assassinations, blackmailing, mob violence, kidnapping and the destruction of public buildings. It contained a section on the "Selective Use of Violence," and advised that, "If possible professional criminals will be used to carry out selective jobs."

The United States was ultimately condemned by the World Court of Justice at the Hague which ruled that, "the United States of America, by training, arming, equipping, financing and supplying the contra forces or otherwise encouraging, supporting and aiding military and paramilitary activities in and against Nicaragua, has acted…in breach of its obligation under customary international law not to intervene in the affairs of another state." This ruling was dismissed outright by the government of the United States, which felt under no obligation to operate within the boundaries of international law.

The ostensible reason for these policies was the supposed containment of Communism. Again, the historic record tells a completely different story. The possibility of true democracy spreading throughout the poor and peasant populations of Central and South America was to be thwarted and suppressed. The entire region was deemed a vital interest, and the countries involved were expected to remain subservient to purely American interests. The nature of this relationship remains true to this day.

This claim that the real motivation for American interventionist behavior is to exert economic power and preserve economic hegemony, is given even more credence by the fact that a month after the fall of the Berlin Wall (November of 1989) and the collapse of the Soviet Union, the United States invaded Panama. This invasion left hundreds, if not thousands, of poor Panamanians dead and destroyed poor neighborhoods leaving the residences of the wealthy very much intact. The pretext of thwarting the spread of Communism could no longer be applied to this military action.

No assessment of the rationale behind American foreign policy in regards to our neighbors to the South would be complete without an examination of our policies towards Cuba. No examination of the current situation would give the full picture without looking at the conditions on the island of Cuba before the Cuban revolution brought Fidel Castro to power.

United States historical documents show that Cuba was seen as a "slave country" or "black country." In 1824, there were plans for a united Mexican-Columbian expedition to free both Cuba and Puerto Rico from Spanish control. The Secretary of State, Henry Clay, was sent as an envoy to dissuade the governments of Mexico and Columbia from taking such a course of action. It was felt that Cuba and Puerto Rico should remain under Spanish domination. The maintenance of Spanish control of the region was obviously viewed as compatible with American interests. This attitude would change dramatically by the end of the century.

In 1897, J.C. Breckenridge, the Undersecretary of War, referring to the blockade enforced around the island of Cuba, commented that, "even if this means using the methods Divine Providence used on the cities of Sodom and Gomorrah, we must impose a harsh blockade, so that hunger and its constant companion, disease, undermine the peaceful population...." These are prophetic words given the harsh sanctions currently imposed on the Cuban people (and the people of Iraq for over twelve years at the cost of the lives of over half of a million children).

The United States military took possession of Guantanamo Bay in early 1898 just after war was declared on Spain. The contract subsequently drawn up by the then U.S.-controlled government of Cuba in 1902 granted an indefinite lease to the United States. In 1903, the Platt Amendment subsequently gave the U.S. control of the Cuban government and society and granted the U.S. the right to effectively intervene in the internal affairs of Cuba at will. According to Article III of this amendment: "The government of Cuba consents that the United States may exercise the right to intervene for the preservation of Cuban independence, the maintenance of government adequate for the protection of life, property, and individual liberty, and for discharging the obligations with respect to Cuba imposed by the Treaty of Paris on the United States, now to be assumed and undertaken by the Government of Cuba...." An end result of these developments was to give the U.S. complete control of Cuba.

From 1933 to 1952, Cuba was ruled by Batista, a brutal dictator supported by the United States. In Batista's Cuba, the economic holdings of American corporate interests were substantial. It was Batista's flagrant disregard for the civil rights and the economic plight of the Cuban people that led to the revolution that brought Fidel Castro to power in 1952.

Fidel immediately came out of favor with the United States government when he embraced socialism and expropriated foreign (i.e. American) holdings in Cuba. Not only did he thwart American economic control of Cuba, but was seen as a threat to American domination over the rest of the region. This threat was in part true, but greatly exaggerated.

After the failure of the U.S. sponsored invasion of Cuba that lead to the fiasco at the Bay of Pigs, the Kennedy administration approved an assassination and terrorist campaign against Cuba referred to as "Operation Mongoose." Throughout the sixties terrorist attacks were aimed at oil refineries, Cuban fishing boats and merchant ships as well as numerous assassination attempts against Fidel Castro. This policy became so extreme that Sam Giancana (a known mafia don) was offered $150,000 for the assassination of Fidel.

There has been an economic blockade imposed upon Cuba since 1960. This has caused untold and needless suffering for the Cuban people, and has remained essentially ineffective. To add to the utter brutality and the extreme short sightedness of this policy towards Cuba, new information has been released about a proposal by the U.S. military (1962) to carry out acts of terrorism against American interests and property in order to drag the United States into war with Cuba by galvanizing public opinion towards such action. The documents that describe this proposal were released by the National Archives within the past few years. The terrorism plan was referred to as "Operation Northwoods." This strategy was ultimately rejected by President Kennedy, and although all pertinent documents were to be destroyed, some were overlooked and later discovered.

This series of blatantly criminal activities directed against the Cuban government and its people is yet just another example of the real focus of U.S. foreign policy: to preserve and extend American economic hegemony in whatever part of the globe that involves American corporate interests, using whatever means necessary. Any attempt to portray the behavior of the U.S. towards other countries as directed by moral obligation and democratic principles is to fly in the face of reality. The fact that a large percentage of the American public seems to accept this interpretation is extremely disquieting. The powerful have become very adept at exploiting the need of individual citizens to feel they belong to and are propelled by the larger ideas and beliefs embodied in "nation."

The other area of intense political engagement was and continues to be the Middle East. Suffice it to say that the overriding concern is the access to cheap oil. The American economy has been driven, especially since the end of the Second World War, by the idea of perpetual material progress fueled by increased production and consumption of commercial goods. This economic model requires the ever increasing expenditure of energy. Although the U.S. represents about 5 percent of the world's population, it consumes some 40 percent of the world's energy resources. It has been estimated that if every individual on the planet lived at the same level of consumption as Americans, four additional planets would be necessary to accommodate that consumption. The cheapest form of energy continues to be oil. This is partly due to the refusal of a succession of government administrations to adequately subsidize and encourage the use of alternative forms of energy including solar and wind power. Any threat to the supply of oil, therefore, threatens the vitality of the economic engine, the wealth of the powerful ruling class and, by inference, the workers who are dependent upon them for their livelihoods. This is, of course, can not be tolerated.

The peoples of the Middle East have been exploited and manipulated by Western colonial powers for many years to ensure their continued unfettered access to oil. The historic record is replete with not so subtle proofs of this assertion. In 1953, the Iranian Premier, Mohammed Mossadeq was overthrown and replaced by the Shah, who was reinstated. The CIA was deeply involved in the plot to unseat Mossadeq in an operation referred to as Ajax. The Premier was deemed to be a threat on account of his leftist political leanings. The Anglo-Iranian Oil Company was expelled from the country some nine months earlier. According to Kermit Roosevelt in his book entitled, *Countercoup: the Struggle for the Control of Iran,* (this book was deemed so "dangerous" that McGraw Hill was persuaded by British Petroleum to recall all the books from the book stores) Anglo-Iranian Oil proposed the overthrow of the Iranian premier.

In the introduction of the *London Draft of the TPAJAX Operational Plan* it is stated that, "The policy of both the U.S. and U.K. governments required replacement of Mossadeq as the alternative to certain economic collapse in Iran and the eventual loss of the area to the Soviet orbit. Only through planned and controlled replacement can the integrity and independence of the country be ensured.

"The plan which follows is comprised of three successive stages. The first two stages precede action of a military nature. They include the present preliminary support period and the mass propaganda campaign. These stages will be of real value to the mutual interests of U.S and U.K. even if final military action is not carried out in that they will make the position of Mossadeq increasingly vulnerable and unsteady."

This plan goes on to state that, "…the United States and the United Kingdom have common aims towards Iran, and that both want to support him (the Shah) to the utmost in opposing Mossadeq."

These documents, and the events that followed from the policies they outlined, are an unambiguous demonstration of the conspiracy on behalf of the United States and the United Kingdom to shape the political landscape of the Middle East to further their own economic interests.

Let us look at one especially timely example, Iraq and its leader Saddam Hussein. This man has been depicted as the veritable incarnation of evil. This is an image presented to the public by various U.S. administrations and promulgated by the media. It is essential that the proponents of war demonize and dehumanize the enemy so as to make it easier for the susceptible population to accept the slaughter and decimation of those who are deemed dangerous. Many examples of Saddam's evil treachery have been cited including his use of poison gas against the Kurds in Northern Iraq. This is undeniablely true when taken by itself, yet, in fact, he was considered an important ally of the United States at the very time this heinous act was taking place. There were no cries of outrage or threats of retaliation at the time. Why would this be the case? Iraq was involved in a terrible war with Iran at that time. The United States was busy giving Iraq access to satellite reconnaissance and other logistical support. The motivation for this support was most likely based on the strategy of divide and conquer, so wondrously perfected by the British during the height of its colonial power. Helping to support and sustain such a terrible conflict weakened both regimes. Keeping the peoples of the region so engaged in regional hatreds and conflicts, distracts them from the realization that they are being exploited by external powers.

Let us examine the proclaimed rationale for our brutal destruction of Iraq during the First Iraq War. Prior to the Iraqi invasion of Kuwait, Saddam had a meeting with American Ambassador, April Glaspie. At this meeting, Saddam intimated to the ambassador his intentions of invading Kuwait. Her response was that it was a completely regional issue outside of the American purview. Given this information, one could question why the American government reacted as it did. Are we to believe that the Ambassador spoke without instruction from the State Department? That is an extremely unlikely possibility.

There is evidence that the United States had a plan to invade Iraq and take control of the oil fields that was drafted in late 1989 or early 1990. The CIA, under the direction of William Webster, assisted Kuwait in its violations of OPEC oil production agreements possibly for the purpose of undercutting the price of oil thus depleting Iraq's economy, in taking illegal amounts of oil from that which it shared with Iraq, and in demanding repayment of loans it had made to Iraq during the Iran-Iraq war. It is not unreasonable to presume that the underlying reason for this behavior was to provoke Iraq into taking action against neighboring Kuwait.

The American response to Iraq's invasion and occupation of Kuwait, once it took place, entailed nothing less than the wholesale destruction of the infrastructure of Iraq. The Iraqis had no real means to defend themselves against the military resources and capabilities of a gigantic superpower. Sixteen of the eighteen power stations were destroyed along with water purification and sewage treatment facilities. This, of course, wrecked havoc on the civilian population. Vast areas of the country, including Baghdad, were subjected to severe and relentless bombardment from the air as well as from cruise missiles launched from many miles off shore. This produced no end of psychological, emotional and physical suffering for the peoples of Iraq. It has been estimated that 80,000 Iraqis lost their lives during the first month of the conflict.

In addition, shells made of depleted uranium (DU) were used and tested in combat situations within Iraq. DU is a highly toxic and radioactive product of the uranium enrichment process. The nuclear industry has in excess of 1.1 billion pounds of DU. It is quite informative that the nuclear industry provided this material free to the munitions factories that manufacture the shells containing DU. This material interested the military for a number of reasons: it is extremely dense and therefore a potent weapon, it exists in huge quantities and could be provided free to the manufacturers of arms. In regards to its deleterious affects on the human body, government documents have made the following admission, "If DU enters the body, it has the potential to generate significant medical consequences. The risks associated with DU in the body are both chemical and radiological."

Depleted uranium is about 60 percent as radioactive as naturally occurring uranium. It has a half-life of 4.5 billion years which means that in that staggering period of time only half of the material would have been reduced naturally to non-radioactive by-products. This, of course, means that any contamination of the environment with DU is permanent. In early tests conducted in the 1970's, the U.S. military began to explore how DU might be used in weaponry. As a result of these tests, it was found that large and small caliber rounds made of DU were highly effective in piercing armor, and could also be incorporated into tank armor to make tanks more impervious to enemy fire. One may wonder whether another motive for developing such weapons might be to reduce the burden of the nuclear industry's vast inventory of this toxic material.

It has been estimated that by the end of the Gulf War, between 40 and 300 tons of depleted uranium were scattered on Iraqi battlefields, especially in the South. There has been a marked increase in the incidence of childhood cancers among Iraqi children predominantly in that region, and also mysterious cases of swollen abdomens. The real health danger of this material results from incorporation into the body. When a DU shell strikes a hard surface, about 70 percent of the material is oxidized and scattered as small particles. Of these particles, 60 percent are less than five microns, a size that can be readily taken in with the breath.

Iraqi civilians, soldiers and American troops came into contact with DU in a variety of ways. There has been more and more evidence suggesting that the so-called "Gulf War Syndrome" may be related to DU exposure. The government has consistently denied any connection between the Gulf War Syndrome and DU. It should be remembered that almost half of the troops in the Gulf were Black and Latino, many of them seeking the military as an employer of last resort. It is the poor, after all, that do the suffering and dying in times of war. Many of them return home not only with both physical and psychological injuries from the conflict, but also with the prospect of suffering from debilitating and chronic illnesses.

The fact that the Pentagon and the Government approved of the use of such a weapon, when its deleterious environmental effects are widely known and understood, is reminiscent of the use of anti-personnel weapons, napalm and Agent Orange in Vietnam. These are patently criminal acts that have escaped punishment only because they have been perpetrated by a rogue nation that believes that its overwhelming military power precludes it from prosecution by agencies of international justice. This was made abundantly clear when the United States ignored the judgment of the World Court in regards to its behavior in Nicaragua during the Reagan presidency. The United States has shown that it is capable of going to violent extremes to achieve political goals unavailable by any other means.

The majority of the American public remain indifferent to these criminal acts and apathetic or callously unsympathetic to their disturbing consequences. Somehow the victims of technological warfare applied on such a momentous scale are not to be viewed with concern, because they have been successfully categorized as the evil enemy and regarded as somehow less than human. This would explain why the events of September 11, 2001 were viewed with such moral outrage while the far greater scale of violence perpetrated against the people of Iraqi has been so passively accepted. There remains to this day a strong public resistance to accept any connection between the horrendous terrorist attack on American soil, and the suffering and death that we are clearly and unmistakably responsible for. It is of no surprise that Saddam Hussein will be tried as a war criminal, while George Bush Sr., his son George W. Bush, Colon Powell, and the other architects of this deadly policy are portrayed as heroes.

This war against Iraq was touted as a UN action, when, in fact, it was predominantly a United States led conflict waged against a weak enemy with little capability to counter such an onslaught. United States troops suffered very few casualties mostly resulting from friendly fire. During this conflict, the American public was subjected to film and video clips showing the wondrous accuracy of so-called "smart weapons." Audiences applauded as buildings, of supposed strategic importance, were blown up, as if no one was inside those buildings as they shattered and were engulfed in flames. The pilots delivering this devastation all returned safely to their bases, for there were no Iraqi defenses to speak of. Military spokesmen described civilian casualties as "collateral damage." It was said that these deaths were a result of accidents rather than bad or malicious intention. This explanation is patent nonsense, for the military was intent on keeping American casualties at a minimum regardless of the human cost to the enemy. The architects of this strategy were wondrously successful, or so they believed and continue to believe.

The Persian Gulf War and the air war against Serbia have shown the extent to which the United States and its Western allies have perfected the art of industrial warfare. This kind of warfare is carried on by mechanized weapons that can destroy large numbers of people and infrastructure from great distances, keeping the perpetrators safe and insulated from the destruction and harvest of death. This kind of warfare has been adeptly described by Chris Hedges, a foreign correspondent, in his timely book entitled, *War is a Force that Gives Us Meaning.*

Although the Gulf War was over in a matter of months, the victor was not satisfied with the suffering that had been imposed. The Iraqi people were made to suffer for an additional twelve years under draconian sanctions that essentially kept them in a state of severe poverty in an environment where the public health facilities were completely devastated. It has been estimated, by a United Nations study, that 500,000 Iraqi children lost their lives as a direct result of these sanctions.

Are these not crimes against humanity? After all, they do not differ qualitatively from the brutal behavior of those defeated in previous wars, who were charged with such crimes and put to death for them. If justice was truly served, Henry Kissinger, George Bush, Colin Powell and General Schwartkof would be put on trial for the murderous crimes they perpetrated against so many people. The nation continues to hold up such leaders with great praise and thankfulness in spite of the needless suffering and devastation they wrecked upon the world for the sake of the powerful. It is conceivable that the truth may ultimately prevail in some future time, when the American empire has waned and its military might is no longer preeminent. Should we really be surprised that much of the world's poor view us with fear, apprehension and hatred?

What was the purpose of such an extreme and brutal response to the invasion of Kuwait? To me the answer is quite obvious: it was a clear demonstration that the United States knows no bounds to its brutality when it feels it has been wronged or its economic hegemony has been threatened. Noam Chomsky in his book, *Rogue States the Rule of Force in World Affairs,* sees this kind of behavior as part of the strategy of an outlaw state that will act unilaterally whenever its own national interests are threatened.

There is a perception in the United States that access to oil from outside its borders is a birthright. It seems entirely antithetical to capitalist precepts to believe that anyone can own something that has not yet been purchased. If the poor man acted based on that philosophy, he would soon be behind bars for a very long time. The powerful can not tolerate their own behavior when it is adopted by the powerless. They know only too well to do so would inevitably lead to their own demise.

A paper was presented to a symposium held by the Albany Law School on February 27, 1992. It was entitled: *International War Crimes: the Search for Justice*. The paper outlines the actions of the George Bush Sr. administration during the Gulf War that would qualify it for war crimes. The charges were made against President George Bush Sr., Vice President Dan Quayle, Secretary of State Jim Baker, Secretary of Defense Dick Cheney, National Security Assistant Brent Scowcroft, CIA Director William Webster, Chairman of the Joint Chiefs of Staff Colin Powell, General Norman Schwarzkopf and other members of the High Command of the United States military establishment.

The charges made against the defendants in this paper were the following, all of which have been documented here and elsewhere:

- Perversion of the U.S. Constitution that clearly and unequivocally gives the Congress and the Congress only the right to declare war.

- Bypassed and violated Chapter VI of the United Nations charter that mandates the specific settlement of the international disputes as is found in Article 2 of the United Nations Charter, claiming that there would be no compromise and no negotiation.

- Destruction of facilities essential to civilian life and economic productivity throughout Iraq. The military targets included business districts, schools, hospitals, mosques, churches, shelters, residential areas, power stations, water purification plants, sewage treatment plants. The estimates range from 25,000 civilian dead to 113,000 including many children. According to the Nuremberg Charter "wanton destruction of cities, towns or villages" is a Nuremberg War Crime. The net result of these atrocities was to leave Iraq with its infrastructure destroyed and its society in a pre-industrial condition. It is estimated that more than 100,000 civilians died from dehydration, dysentery, malnutrition, hunger, shock and distress.

- Wanton killing of Iraqi soldiers with the dead numbering in the tens of thousands. These soldiers were essentially incapable of defending themselves from such a technological assault. Many of these soldiers were buried alive at the beginning of hostilities.

- The use of prohibited weapons of mass destruction. These weapons included fuel air explosives, napalm, cluster bombs and anti-personnel fragmentation bombs used in Basra and so-called "Super bombs" used against hardened shelters. Included among those killed on the "Highway of Death" were civilians of all ages including Kuwaitis, Iraqis, Palestinians, Jordanians and others.

- Military actions clearly endangering the environment.

The atrocities cited in this paper are all a matter of the historic record and can not be reasonably refuted. They point not only to the Bush administration, but to the foreign policy of the United States that has been systematically involved in a brutal war against the poor of this world, whenever they are deemed to pose a threat to America's economic and military expansion.

The drums of war have not yet been stilled. The destruction of the World Trade Center Towers in New York, together with thousands of people who occupied those buildings and lost their lives, the loss of passengers in the four airplanes that were used as weapons and those who died when the Pentagon building was hit, had a profound impact on the American people. Suddenly, we could no longer feel safe within our own borders. Suddenly, we are no longer immune from the violence that besets so many of the world's people. The government, of course, would admit no linkage between this horrendous event and the untold suffering experienced by the Iraqi people as a direct result of our military and economic assault upon them, or the suffering of the Palestinian people at the hands of the Israelis with weapons supplied by the United States. The event was portrayed as an assault by evil doers who feel hatred for the United States on account of the freedom and democracy it affords its people. The United States government, through its many administrations, has never taken responsibility for its brutal and violent behavior throughout the world. It has always assumed that it could attack other nations with extreme brutality and never expect reprisals from its victims abroad. The late Senator Fullbright referred to this attitude as the "Arrogance of Power." The events of September 11 have proven that this viewpoint is mistaken. It is most unfortunate that rather then taking the opportunity to change the course of history, the U.S. has taken the road towards massive retaliation and building a bigger and more impenetrable wall around itself. This, in my mind, is completely wrong headed and ultimately self destructive. It is reminiscent of the attitude and behavior of the Roman Empire before its downfall. Rome at that time was over-extended abroad and collapsing from within. I find many parallels between the Roman Empire and the current state of affairs in the United States with troops all around the world, an enormous defense budget, staggering budget deficits, and many millions of its citizens disenfranchised without adequate health care, housing, education and nutrition. The analogy is reinforced still further by the great divide between the few who have and everyone else.

There has been an ongoing campaign by the George W. Bush administration to establish a policy of continual war, and his administration managed to extract from the Congress a blanket approval for preemptive strikes on whatever sovereignty or power that is deemed to be the enemy of the moment. This represents such a grand distraction from the serious domestic problems that plague ordinary citizens. The society has come to require and accept the presence of an enemy, real or imagined, that is seen as threatening our way of life. America has become apparently incapable of using reason in its dealing with other peoples or nations different than ourselves, and has lost any real sense of humanity. In part, this attitude stems from the racism that lies at the nation's core and is a reflection of how it sees itself. This exceedingly arrogant and prejudicial way of looking at the world at large is filled with unintended consequences that may eventually lead to the down-fall of the empire, most probably from within. One need only examine the current size of the military budget and the state of the national economy with a staggering budget deficit (greater than 500 billion dol-lars). More and more resources are now destined to fill the coffers of the war industries for the manufacture of exquisite machines of death at the expense of health care, education, adequate housing and nutri-tion for many Americans. Much of the infrastructure of the country is in a serious state of decline and will go on being neglected with the cur-rent emphasis on "national security."

One of the first acts of reprisals for September 11 was the war against Afghanistan and especially Osam Bin Laden, Al Qaeda and the Taliban leadership that had supposedly been protecting them. Not only has this war failed to find or capture Osama Bin Laden, but it has led to the death of many innocent civilians with some estimates put at around 3,500 individuals by human rights advocates. This is not counting the thousands of refugees from the bombing who faced imminent starvation.

A documentary film entitled, *Massacre in Mazar*, was made by the Irish director, Jamie Doran. The film presents testimony from Afghan eye witnesses that U.S. troops participated in the torture and murder of thousands of Taliban prisoners near Mazar-i-Sharif. This film received widespread coverage in the European press, and, not surprisingly, almost no coverage in the United States. This apparent censorship on the part of the domestic press is yet another example of how the corporate media has cooperated with the government in distilling and filtering the news reaching the American people.

One might ask why Afghanistan was so brutally attacked. Were there any other considerations that were not within the public eye? In December 2000, the Department of Energy reported that, "Afghanistan's significance from an energy standpoint stems from its geographical position as a potential transit route for oil and natural gas exports from Central Asia to the Arabian Sea." Unocal, one of the promoters of a natural gas pipeline through Afghanistan determined that the "Centgas" pipeline project would not be feasible without an internationally recognized government in Afghanistan. In February of 1998, John J. Maresca, Vice President of International Relations at Unocal, testified in front of the House Committee on International Relations Subcommittee on Asia and the Pacific. In his testimony, he stated that, "Today, we would like to focus on three issues concerning this region, its resources and U.S. policy. The need for multiple pipeline routes for Central Asian oil and gas. The need for U.S. support for international regional efforts to achieve balanced and lasting political settlements with Russia, other newly independent states and in Afghanistan. The need for structured assistance to encourage economic reforms and the development of appropriate investment climates in the region...."

Furthermore, the U.S. has a seventy percent interest in the recoverable oil reserves in Kazakhstan. It should be remembered that the current Vice President, Dick Cheney was the CEO of Dallas-based Halliburton Co., the largest oil services company in the world. Cheney was reported to have said to a group of oil industry executives in 1998 that, "I can't think of a time when we've had a region emerge as suddenly to become as strategically important as the Caspian."

This information suggests that economic interests contributed to the decision to invade Afghanistan and, in so doing, establish an economic and military presence in that region of the world. Poor nations endowed with plentiful natural resources and geographic importance invariably become the focus of the colonial powers.

This plan finally came to fruition after the fall of the Taliban. On December 27, 2002, the British Broadcasting Company (BBC) reported, in an article entitled *Central Asia Pipeline Deal Signed*, that an agreement had been signed in Ashgabat, the Turkman capital, that prepared for the construction of a gas pipeline from Turkman through Afghanistan to Pakistan.

The repeated attempts by the George W. Bush administration to justify its behavior on moral grounds, portraying the nation as a defender of freedom and democracy, is made particularly ludicrous when juxtaposed with its policies towards the State of Israel. Israel has brutally occupied what is left of the Palestinian homeland (approximately twenty-two percent of what it was pre-1948) for over thirty-five years. It has continuously used collective punishment (a technique that was perfected by the Nazis) to contain the population and suppress any real possibility of statehood. Some of the methods that it has employed include: demolition of homes, destruction of Palestinian agricultural land (especially the olive groves), keeping huge portions of the population under house arrest, rationing water, destruction of infrastructure, imposed unemployment by making it literally impossible for workers to leave their homes, obstructing access to health care, outright assassinations of political leaders of all persuasions, the use of live ammunition against women, children, the old and the infirm, and the imposition of numerous roadblocks and checkpoints making the conducting of everyday business nearly impossible. In 2003, Israel had completed the first phase of their plan to build a huge impenetrable wall around Palestinian lands. The Israelis control movement through the fortress gates of this wall, and have effectively cut off whole communities from access to their agricultural lands and most importantly to water. The residents of the Jewish settlements have access to five times the amount of water per person than the Palestinians even though the Palestinians have legal rights to it. It has used these brutal methods while at the same time maintaining and expanding Jewish settlements in the Palestinian territories. The residents of these settlements enjoy all the benefits and comforts of an affluent society in spite of the poverty and desperation that surrounds them. It seems obvious that the rationale behind these actions is to create a de-facto situation that would preclude the possibility of ever having a viable and contiguous Palestinian state. The Israeli people have likewise suffered from the behavior of their government in that the conditions of deprivation and oppression of the Palestinians has nurtured the growth of extremist Palestinian factions. These groups have used suicide bombers to unleash their rage in a terribly destructive and deadly fashion. The Israeli people have also suffered from the deleterious psychological effects that come from the unrelenting and brutal occupation of Palestinian land and people.

The State of Israel continues to deny it has a nuclear arsenal. In early 1968, the CIA reported that Israel had successfully started production of nuclear weapons. By 1974, it was estimated that Israel had between ten and twenty nuclear bombs. As of 2002, estimates are that Israel has up to two hundred nuclear weapons and the missiles to deliver them. Current evidence also suggests that the Israeli military now has in its possession submarines armed with nuclear weapons. In spite of all of this, the U.S. Administration fully supports the Israeli agenda both politically and financially. Some of this financial support is being used to finance the building of the Palestinian wall.

Successive U.S. governments used their veto power in the United Nations Security Council to effectively block the enforcement of numerous resolutions passed in regard to the Palestinian territories. No attempt was ever made to send inspectors to Israel to uncover their weapons of mass destruction. One wonders what happened to the U.S. commitment to democracy and freedom. The reason for this glaring inconsistency in policy is patently obvious. Israel is a crucial ally in the region where the United States has so many enemies. Israel's predominant role is to maintain stability in the region by sheer force and the threat of force. If nuclear weapons were ever used, it is either Israel or the Unites States that is most likely to use them. They are, in fact, the real rogue powers on the planet, and the ones to be feared and mistrusted.

Soon after the Taliban regime was successfully toppled in Afghanistan and a government favorable to U.S. interests was put in place, The United States turned its attention to Iraq once again. The United States military amassed 150,000 troops on Iraq's borders and had begun clamoring for war, attempting to pressure the Security Council of the United Nations to go along with this aggression supposedly to disarm Saddam Hussein. The rhetoric coming from the administration at the time was that regardless of the Security Council's decision, the United States would invade for the purpose of uncovering and destroying weapons of mass destruction. This rationale was proven to be patently false. The intention was to overthrow Saddam Hussein's government and install a "democracy" which, in fact, meant placing individuals into powerful positions who would be beholding to the United States, and ready to insure the U.S. an economic and military foothold in the country. Iraq is known to have a vast amount of undeveloped oil reserves. Keep in mind that Halliburton, the energy development company that was once chaired by Vice President Richard Cheney, stands to harvest great profits from oil development and reconstruction in Iraq

I was hopeful that such a war could be avoided for many reasons. Primarily, such a one-sided conflict, where technological weapons would be used extensively, would lead to the unnecessary suffering and death of many Iraqis. This "war" would be regarded by many people around the world as a blatant act of imperialist aggression by a superpower against an essentially defenseless country. Furthermore, Iraq had already been decimated by the very same country who views itself as its liberator. Passions ran so high against the war that millions of citizens throughout the world participated in street protests even before the invasion began. My fear was that the level of hatred and distrust against the United States would grow substantially if the invasion took place.

If this militaristic approach to dealing with international problems continues, it could lead to an ever increasing and expanding escalation of violence world wide. This scenario can be avoided if the United States government and its people radically change their behavior at home and abroad, and begin to peacefully cooperate with other nations for the purpose of solving the endemic problems of hunger, housing, health and well being. This change would require becoming a real member of the community of nations and represent a desire to rethink policies based on purely economic self interest.

Unfortunately, war was not prevented. As a matter of fact, the administration, using Colon Powel as its spokesman, attempted to make its case for war to the United Nations Security Council. The evidence that was presented regarding supposed weapons of mass destruction was weak and unconvincing at best and outright fraudulent at worst. France, Russia and China did not accept this evidence as convincing. Rather than face a veto of the resolution that it placed before the Security Council, the United State met with its allies, Great Britain and Spain, and acted unilaterally. George W. Bush offered an ultimatum to the Iraqi government: either abdicate or suffer the consequences. In that way, international law was rendered useless in the face of awesome military strength, and a dangerous precedent was set for any nation to take pre-emptive military action against a state that it might view as inimical to its interests. A grossly illegal war was waged, using overwhelming military force against a weak government eviscerated by twelve years of sanctions that was responsible for the death of hundreds of thousands.

The war, itself, was responsible for the deaths of thousands of civilians (the current estimate is some 9000 people) as well as Iraqi soldiers, whose death toll probably rose to the tens of thousands. An example of the extent of brutality and horror perpetrated by American forces is given by the eye witness account of Robert Fisk who writes, "There was a fearful battle along Highway 1 on the western bank of the Tigris river in which Hussein's guerillas fought off an American tank column for 36 hours, the U.S. tanks spraying shellfire down a motorway until every vehicle—military and civilian—was a smoldering wreck. I walked the highway as the last shots were still being fired by snipers, peering into cars packed with the blackened corpses of men, women, children.

"Carpets and blankets had been thrown over several piles of the dead. In the back of one car lay a young, naked woman, her perfect features blackened by fire, her husband or father still sitting at the steering wheel, his legs severed below his knees.

"It was a massacre. Did we think the Iraqis would forget it?"

All of these victims had parents, spouses, children and siblings who are not likely to forget any time soon. To expect the Iraqi people to embrace the very people that visited upon them so much death and needless suffering is ludicrous at best. The North is now dominated by the Kurds, who are beginning their own policy of ethnic cleansing. Baghdad and the cities of the south were initially overwhelmed by chaos, looting and death. The people of Iraq were faced with a scarcity of essential commodities, ailing hospitals and inadequate health care. The city of Baghdad suffered from power outages and unemployment is still exceedingly high. The main objectives of the occupying forces are to suppress political unrest and protect the oil fields, while the diplomats seek to insure that a government is put into place that will be subservient to U.S. interests. An Associated Press report from Baghdad dated April 18, 2003, stated that, "Since US forces rolled into central Baghdad a week ago, one of the sole public buildings untouched by looters has been Iraq's massive oil ministry, which is under round-the-clock surveillance by troops." Iraq is probably faced with many years of military occupation.

If one were to follow the money, the meaning of all of this becomes quite clear. Billions of American taxpayer dollars have been used to finance the destruction of Iraq over the last twelve years. Once the Iraqi regime was successfully overthrown and supplanted with the American occupation, private corporate interests such as Halliburton and Bechtel were awarded exclusive contracts for reconstruction and oil development projects and stand to harvest the profits.

According to Iraqi law, prior to the occupation, foreign nationals were not permitted to invest in the establishment of, or to acquire stock in an Iraqi company. The Iraq constitution also forbids the privatization of state assets. However, on September 19, 2003, Paul Bremer, the Administrator of the Coalition Provisional Authority (CPA), authorized the implementation of Order Number 39. This order ratified the privatization of 200 Iraqi companies, and decreed that foreign firms can acquire 100% ownership of Iraqi banks, mines and factories. It also permitted these foreign investors to move 100% of their profits out of the country. This wholesale abrogation of Iraqi law is clearly in violation of international law. The Hague regulations state that an occupying force must honor "unless absolutely prevented, the laws in force in the country."

It is clear that the process of what is referred to as "reconstruction" represents the wholesale transfer of ownership of the energy and productive capacity of an entire nation into the hands of essentially American corporate interests. Privatization of Iraqi business is now occurring on a grand scale with the major benefactors being those who contributed substantially to the George W. Bush presidency. Even the school textbooks are being published in the United States. All this is being done without any measurable input from the Iraqi people. This represents a radical attempt to re-engineer an entire culture into a prototype designed to fulfill American interests and to further feed the voracious appetite of capitalism in its hunger for new markets. In reality, however, it is a strategy that has incurred considerable costs in regard to the suffering endured by the Iraqi people and the American military, that functions as a mere pawn in the game of power.

The coercive practices of the international economic institutions such as the International Monetary Fund (IMF), World Bank and the World Trade Organization (WTO) are being met with considerable resistance throughout the world. Iraq represents an entirely new model for economic development in which a country is first destroyed and then rebuilt from the debris, circumventing completely the cumbersome problems that sovereignty brings.

Not only have no weapons of mass destruction been found, but there is no longer talk of their existence. It's as if they were never an issue to begin with. All the accumulated evidence points to the magnitude of the deception that was foisted upon the American public, for the purpose of pursuing this course of action. It is certainly behavior worthy of impeachment.

At the end of June, 2004, the U.S. allegedly handed over sovereignty to the Iraqis. This accounting of what actually transpired is misleading. In fact, Paul Bremer left his position after transferring limited authority to a handpicked Iraqi leadership. The U.S. has over 140,000 troops and permanent military bases in the country. Furthermore, new Iraqi laws have been crafted, by the occupying authority, that directly benefit and maintain U.S. political and economic hegemony, as previously described. This is a sovereignty of a very dubious kind.

With this phase of the conflict over, the administration turned its attention to the Palestinian issue. A so-called "Road Map for Peace" was drafted by the United States, Russia, the European Union and the United Nations. Israeli President Ariel Sharon claimed that it is probably time for the Palestinians and Israel to divide up the territories. This is an interesting perspective given these are the territories that the state of Israel has been occupying for over thirty-five years. None of it belongs to the Israelis. It is theirs by the use of overwhelming and brutal force not unlike the tactics of the Nazis during the Second World War. Absurdly, this is seen as a concession to the peace process. This Road Map does not call for the complete dismantling of Israeli settlements in the West Bank. Without this concession, the creation of the State of Palestine, which is the stated goal of the plan, could never result in a contiguous state with defined borders without losing a large amount of territory to the settlements. The Road Map does not call for the destruction of the wall that the Israelis are building. This wall has effectively decreased Palestinian lands and separated the Palestinians from much of their olive vineyards. A supposed concession made by the Israelis for the sake of peace is the dismantling of illegal settlements which represent some tents or trailers. Even this meager gesture has met with considerable resistance from the Israeli settlements. Meanwhile, the Israelis continue their policy of extra-legal assassinations of the militant Palestinian opposition.

In April of 2004, Sharon met with George W. Bush. At the meeting, Sharon shared his new proposal with Bush. That proposal was that all Jewish settlements would be moved out of Gaza. Certain settlements in the West Bank would be retained and the wall would continue to be built. In reality, the settlements in Gaza are small and exceedingly fragile, since the Israeli settlers are heavily outnumbered by Palestinians. As a consequence of that meeting, George W. Bush claimed, at the subsequent news briefing, that, "…realities on the ground dictated that Israel should be able to keep some settlements in the any future peace agreement." This overt approval by Bush of the Israeli plan effectively sabotaged any chance for a resolution of major concerns voiced by the Palestinians, scuttled United Nations Resolutions 242, 348 and undermined any hope of reaching the stated goals of the Road Map.

In my judgment, the most disturbing aspect of this upheaval and conflict in the Middle East is the callous indifference of many Americans, who viewed the Second Gulf War and its aftermath as a kind of bizarre entertainment. The unsettling images of the massive bombardment and overwhelming lethal force used against a vastly overwhelmed enemy was treated as if the enemy was less than human. The flags were brought out and patriotism was invoked, in spite of the fact that the U.S. was clearly the aggressor in this conflict. The profoundly devastating effect all this violence has on the American public, especially the young, is difficult to quantitate but disturbing to contemplate. In her book entitled *Power Politics*, Arundhati Roy referred to Americans as, "a curiously insular people, administered by the pathologically meddlesome, promiscuous government."

Exactly how has this insularity been maintained in a rapidly shrinking world? Corporate interests and the military establishment, together with the help and resourcefulness of the media, exert considerable influence over the social order and custom in America. A noteworthy trend in recent years has been growth of the media conglomerates. In 1983, fifty corporations dominated the mass media. As of this writing, the *Nation* reported that there are ten corporations (mostly American) that dominate the media in the year 2003. These are: AOL-Times Warner, Disney, Bartelsmann, Vivendi, Viacom, New Corporation, AT&T, General Electric (owner of NBC), Sony and Liberty Media. The danger inherent in this trend is that the dissemination of news is under the control of fewer and fewer sources. Many of these conglomerates are essentially entertainment industries that have become vertically integrated and whose major preoccupation is profit. Michael Eisner, CEO of the Disney Corporation, stated in a now famous memo, "We have no obligation to make history. We have no obligation to make a statement. To make money is our only objective."

These giant companies are essentially politically conservative in outlook. They benefit from the existing socio-economic order not only in the United States but around the world on account of their global reach. It is not likely that they will look kindly upon social and political upheavals around the world that might pose a threat to the status quo, and would, therefore, do their utmost to suppress this information. This is not an idle concern, for there are many instances in which newsworthy events have been either under reported or not reported at all. One example being the conflict with Afghanistan, as cited earlier. There was no real examination of America's economic interests in the region, the close ties between the Osama Bin Laden and the Reagan administration during the Soviet occupation of Afghanistan and the extent of the suffering endured by the Afghanistan people as a direct result of the invasion. How many of the poor actually died of starvation during the invasion? How many innocent civilians were victims of the bombardment? How many people became permanent refugees? These are the questions that journalists should attempt to address.

Another example includes the under reporting of the daily suffering imposed on the Palestinian people by the Israeli government. It is only the Palestinian suicide bombings that get the extensive coverage. In contrast, the daily humiliation, harassment and killings of the Palestinian people by the Israeli occupation are rarely commented on. This imbalance in reporting is not accidental. It creates the impression that the Israelis, who are occupying Palestinian lands, are simply the victims of unprovoked attacks by Palestinian terrorists.

There are many other instances of this selective coverage of events. The extent of civilian causalities in Serbia as a result of U.S. and NATO bombing raids was not adequately covered. The death of civilians at the hands of NATO forces was viewed as "collateral damage" resulting from human error, and, therefore, apparently of no real importance. Another grievous example was the almost complete blackout of coverage regarding the U.S. supported invasion of East Timor in 1975 by the Indonesian government and subsequent massacre of hundreds of thousands of East Timorese. Henry Kissinger was directly implicated in the U.S. involvement in this affair. If it were not for the persistent exposure of this aggression by the likes of Naom Chomskey, the details of these atrocities might never have been revealed.

The agenda of the powerful is, of course, to remain in power. The fact that the day to day business of the media in reporting the news has been ceded to powerful interests is and should be disquieting. How can ordinary citizens make reasoned and informed decisions about major developments in the world without fair, adequate and full disclosure of events as they unfold? Instead, the news that reaches the public is often pre-digested and made to conform to self-serving principles. This is what makes government propaganda so effective, for it has the backing of the global media conglomerates.

The United States emerged from the Second World War with the largest and most robust economy. Much of this prosperity was a direct result of growth of the military-industrial complex, a term originally coined by the late President Eisenhower. The military defense budget in 2002 was 350 billion dollars. This figure may soar to a staggering 500 billion dollars by 2003 on account of the war against Iraq. In 1995, the U.S. spent $264 billion dollars on the military, or 40 percent of the military expenditure of the entire world. A considerable portion of this budget is used for outright subsidies to defense contractors. The weapons are manufactured by corporations, but much of the financial burden is carried by taxpayers. Part of the job of the Secretary of Defense is to make sales pitches to representatives of foreign governments and to help sell contracts on behalf of corporations such as Boeing and Lockheed. The U.S. is currently the largest arms supplier in the world, selling many billions of dollars worth in 2001. The government has a vested interest in conflicts as they rage across the planet. The investment of so many poor nations in armaments not only diminishes the use of economic resources for their own peoples, but also subsidizes the American arms industry. Violence only begets more violence. The vicious cycle of escalating violence is not helped by the introduction of so many highly technological weapons of mass destruction into the world's arsenals.

Among those who profit directly from both the arms trade and war itself, are many well placed ex-government officials including the senior George Bush. He is intimately involved with the Carlyle Group, an investment company with a stake in defense companies, medical laboratories and telecommunications. Other members of this group include: Joseph Carlucci: Secretary of Defense under Reagan, James Baker: Secretary of State under George Bush, Fidel Ramos: former President of the Philippines and John Major: former Prime Minister of England. It is interesting to note that some of the firm's investors were members of Osama bin Laden's family. The Carlyle Group works within and directly benefits from the close relationships between industry, government and the military.

The development of military technology, the production and sale of military equipment and the maintenance of a standing army, navy and air force, represent a substantive part of the national economy. These expenditures adversely impact needed social programs.

In the shadow of these powerful forces, peace, humanity and freedom remain elusive. Real transformation will only come when people truly unite and insist on and demand change. The forces for change must not be placated by empty promises of reform. The only change that will endure is structural change. The transformation I envision is one in which the nation truly reflects the popular will, and national energy and resources are directed towards establishing economic and social justice. True and lasting peace will come when we begin to treat the peoples of the world with compassion, generosity and humanity, and give up the will to dominate. America would then be perceived as being among the family of nations and not above them. This would entail accepting some profound changes including bringing our consumption of the world's energy and resources into balance. Another change will involve bringing down the fortress we have built up around us and letting more of the world in. We stand to learn a great deal from the differing viewpoints and creative impulses that come from cultures other than our own. The nation must begin the process of healing itself from within. A critical part of this process is to acknowledge and begin to make restitution for the destruction we have wrecked upon the Native American and African American populations and the many peoples throughout the world who have felt the brutal expression of our might. We must begin to lessen our penchant for consumption and invest in renewable sources of energy and planet-friendly production. We must re-channel our resources for the social good and invest in the future of the planet. We must begin to dismantle our staggering inventory of weapons of mass destruction, and encourage all nations to do the same. We must decry the use of space for military purposes. We must pursue a course of true democracy by eradicating the insidious and corrupting link between special interests money and an allegedly representative government. We must bring democracy to the work place and encourage participation of the public in governing and government. We must, in short, begin a process of profound and peaceful change that will transform the United States from a powerful and arrogant empire acting alone in the world in pursuit of its own interests, into one nation among many nations, ready and able to participate fully in eliminating poverty and social and economic injustice throughout the world. Without this kind of transformation, the nation is bound to accelerate its own decline and ultimate demise.

The above list of imperatives will be seen by some as so much wishful thinking. I maintain, however, that these actions must be taken if we want the species to successfully continue into the future. The current path is irrational and essentially self destructive. One does not need a vivid imagination to envision the future if we continue on our present course unabated. We will see a world exhausted of its natural resources and denuded of the marvelous diversity of life that is receding from the planet at an alarming rate. We will see the world of humans plagued by bitter hatreds, antagonisms and endless cycles of wars and violence fueled by the enormous disparity between rich and poor. We can not continue much longer on this path without reaping disastrous consequences.

In the next chapter, we will examine in some detail the extent of the corruption in American corporate structure and practices in an attempt to expose what really exists beneath the blatantly false image of the benevolence of corporate power under the guise of free enterprise.

4

Free Enterprise and the Myth of Prosperity

It is difficult to picture America without commerce. America is insepa-rable from its material culture. Walking down any American main street, I am struck by the unavoidable fact that all life gravitates around what is available for sale. Many of the stores that dominate the market place are the same no matter what city they are in. The airwaves are dominated by buying and selling. So much of ordinary life is occupied with consumption.

The apologists for the American brand of commerce and business represent it as a free enterprise system. Such a description could not be farther from the truth. It is a system dominated by conglomerate cor-porate enterprises that span the ordinary boundaries of nation states. It is yet another myth that can not stand up against the sharp light of scrutiny.

It is important to begin by examining just how the corporation actually came into being, and to try to understand how it came to dominate so much of modern life. The corporation became a legal entity as a result of judicial fiat. In 1886, the Supreme Court was hear-ing arguments in the case of Santa Clara County vs. Southern Pacific Railroad. In its historic decision, the Court held that under the U.S. Constitution a private corporation was a "natural person" entitled to all the rights and privileges afforded to a human being. This decision dramatically altered the character of American society and culture.

From that point on corporations could seek the same legal protections and entitlements normally afforded to ordinary citizens.

Corporations have not only grown in sheer size over the intervening years, but have also subsumed many different kinds of business ventures under a single corporate roof becoming what is referred to as conglomerates. Some examples of these giants are the tobacco companies such as Philip Morris which is now involved in food production among other things, and the oil companies such as Exxon-Mobil. A truly representative example would be that of Gulf + Western which has over 100 companies, under its corporate umbrella, involved in the production of such diverse products as auto parts, musical instruments, cigars, insurance, farm supplies and traffic lights. It operates in every state and in fifty foreign countries. Because of the enormity of their financial holdings and assets, conglomerates wield tremendous political power.

Ben Bagdikian in his book, *The Media Monopoly*, details the breadth and power of the media conglomerates in the United States. At the end of World War II, 80 percent of the nation's newspapers were independently owned. By 1989, 80 percent of the newspapers were owned by corporate chains. By 1987, three corporations controlled the nation's 11,000 magazines. These data are glaring evidence of the consolidation of the media into the hands of a very few, very powerful interests. Furthermore, the corporations that control the print media also are involved in broadcasting, movies, cable and motion pictures. It should be kept in mind that the owners of these media operations also have strong ties to the banking, insurance, oil and defense industries.

Bagdikian examined the growth and business practices of the Gannett Trust, the largest newspaper chain in the United States. The author went on to conclude, "Chain papers are divided in their political drive. Either they pursue the doctrines of their owners, like Freedom or the chains that impose centralized endorsements, or they become bland to avoid controversy. Editorials that take a stand may offend advertisers or community groups. In general, as all organizations become large and directed from afar, they value predictability and beaurecratic smoothness. A *Journalism Quarterly* study of editorials over a fifteen-year period found that after an independent paper is bought by a chain the general result "is not helpful to readers who seek guidance on local matters when they turn to the editorial pages of their daily papers.""

The tendency towards consolidation of the media into the hands of a few powerful interests provides them with enormous political power. With the ability to sway and manipulate public opinion, they can easily make or break political leaders. William Randolph Hearst understood this only too well, having effectively used the press to rouse public support for the Spanish American War. Such power has been abused repeatedly in the past and will most likely intensify in the future. In addition, such concentration of power and influence effectively undermines any possibility of a free market, for broad control of such a wide range of diverse media markets insures that the market place will be manipulated to maximize profit.

Kevin Phillips, in his book entitled *Arrogant Capital*, makes the point that America's ascendancy is in a state of serious decline. He speaks at some length about the "Financialization of America." According to the author, "Finance has not simply been spreading into every nook and cranny of economic life; a sizeable portion of the financial sector, electronically liberated from past constraints, has put aside old concerns with funding the nation's long-range industrial future, has divorced itself from the precarious prospects of Americans who toil in factories, fields, or even suburban shopping malls and is simply feeding wherever it can."

Much of the economic boom of the 1980s and '90s had not been the result of tangible improvements in the real economy, but rather a result of wild speculation in the financial and money markets. Exorbitant returns did not reflect real economic production, but rather a manipulation of the financial markets so that having money, made money. Greed for wealth without necessarily working for it is what drove this process. The bubble finally burst in the 1990s, an event that could have easily been predicted.

From an historic perspective, the concentration of wealth in the hands of the very few is not a new phenomenon. Neither is the close connection between government policies and business interests. Evidence for the corrupting influence of big money upon political institutions is, also, quite evident throughout the nation's history.

In Kevin Phillips' book entitled, *Wealth and Democracy*, the role of wealth in the life of the nation is clearly delineated. America of the twenty-first century is not only the wealthiest nation with the greatest number of very rich individuals, but also the nation with an immense gap between rich and poor. It also stands as a nation with an extremely inadequate social safety net for most of its people.

This gap between the haves and the have nots is not a new aspect of American life. According to Mr. Phillips, "Many of the declaration's signers were representative of America's richest families-a Massachusetts Hancock, a New York Livingston, a Carroll of Maryland, a Lee of Virginia, and a South Carolina Rutledge. Theirs was a revolutionary document with respect to Britain, but not in matters domestic....Hierarchy was a fact of life in the eighteenth-century American colonies."

Throughout the nation's history, enormous power and influence rested in the hands of a very small portion of the population. The current accumulation of wealth by those at the top of the economic pyramid is not very different from the situation in 1890, when the top 1 percent of the population controlled some 50 percent of the entire nation's wealth.

Wealth flowed to those with the closest connection with government, especially in time of war. This relationship remains true to this day with the most recent example being the profits accruing to those companies, such as Bechtel and Halliburton, involved in the reconstruction of Iraq, whose leaders have very close ties to the George W. Bush Administration.

At various times in the nation's history, reform movements, pushing progressive agendas, rose up to oppose the ascendance of the powerful. This momentum for social change was often disrupted by war, for war usually causes a shift of political alignments to the right and, thereby, strengthens the hand of the powerful. This was clearly seen in regard to World War I, which saw the fall of the Progressive movement from its position of strength.

Since the end of World War II, there has been a continual increase in the growth of corporate power and its concomitant impact on American life. At the present time, corporate power dominates national policy both at home and abroad and shapes the lives and destinies of the American people.

The extent of corruption in the corporate culture has been exposed in regard to such companies as Enron, Arthur Anderson, Global Crossing, Tyco, WorldCom, Xerox, Qwest, Merrill Lynch and others. Arianna Huffington has detailed the extent of corporate misconduct in her book, *Pigs at the Trough*. A glaring representation of the real nature of economic life in America is the disparity between the salaries of corporate CEOs and the workers who are responsible for the productive capacity of these industries. Currently, on average, the CEO makes over 500 times the salary of the workers whose destinies they control. Furthermore, between 1990 and 2000, the average pay of a CEO increased by 571 percent, while the average worker's salary has risen only 37 percent over this same time period.

According to Arianna Huffington, "…in the year before Enron collapsed, about 100 executives and energy traders collected more than $300 million dollars in cash payments from the company. More than $100 million dollars went to former CEO Kenneth Lay. After filing bankruptcy, Enron lost $68 billion in market value, 5000 employees lost their jobs and Enron workers lost $800 million from their pension funds." While Enron proved to be a particularly egregious example, it has not been uncommon for CEOs of failing companies to become remarkably enriched at the expense of both their workers and the national economy.

Under the mantle of free enterprise, industries such as airlines, telecommunications and energy have been strong proponents of deregulation, and have influenced and even helped craft legislation to accomplish this goal. Many laws allowing deregulation have already been passed. Such laws have been satisfying to the industries involved, but often injurious to consumers. The net result has been the consolidation of power into the hands of fewer and fewer companies, the telecommunications and airlines industries being notable examples. Thankfully, the Enron debacle exposed the hidden face of deregulation, and hopefully forestalled a rush to deregulation in the energy sector.

The extent to which corporate power has captured the political process can be demonstrated by examining the quantities of money that flow from corporations to legislators in the form of campaign contributions. In the last ten years, the contributions made by corporations to legislators have exceeded 1 billion dollars in so-called "soft money". In fact, there were only two Senators: Thomas Carper (Del.) and Mark Dayton (Minn.) who did not accept campaign contributions from WorldCom, Enron or Arthur Anderson. Furthermore, Enron and its executives gave some $2.4 million dollars to Congressional candidates during the 2000 election and to George W. Bush's campaign as well. In light of this information, it is not surprising that Kenneth Lay was given access and input into the Federal Energy Regulatory Commission (FERC), the very agency charged with regulating the energy industry. This cozy relationship between corporate power and government is not the exception, but the norm. The concentration of power in the hands of a small minority of individuals has apparently been a hallmark of the Republic since its inception. An unmistakable indication of this reality is the actual distribution of wealth.

Current (2002) estimates are that 40 percent of all households have a mere 1 percent of all the wealth in the nation. The top 1 percent holds 30 percent of the total wealth, and the top 20 percent of the population controls 70 percent of the wealth. The extent of this inequity is, in my estimation, staggering in scope. It is a serious indictment of our social order that so few have so much, while so many can barely sustain themselves economically. A graphic representation of the distribution of wealth is shown below (Chart 2).

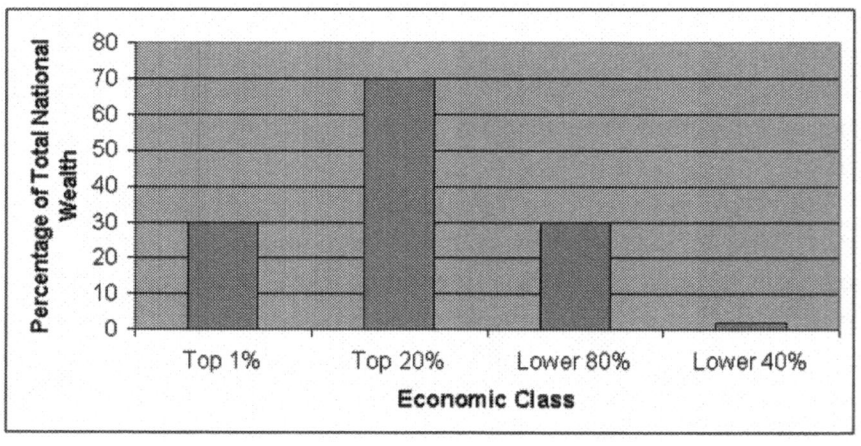

Chart 2 The Distribution of Total National Wealth among the Economic Classes

In addition, the distribution of household income shows that the top 20 percent of the wealthiest individuals have over 10 times as much household income than those individuals that comprise the lower 20 percent. These data are represented graphically below (Chart 3).

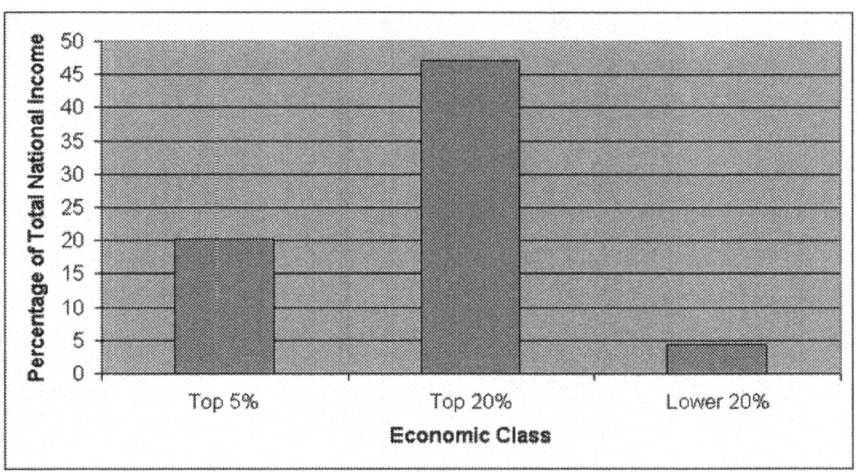

Chart 3 The Distribution of Total National Income among the Economic Classes

These statistics indicate, without any doubt, that an overwhelming share of the nation's economic resources lies in the hands of a very few. These facts, of course, are opened to wide range of interpretations. A particularly interesting interpretation was proposed in an article entitled, *Understanding the U.S. Distribution of Wealth*, written by Vincenzo Quadrinia and Jose-Victor Rios-Rull, which appeared in the Federal Reserve Bank of Minneapolis Quarterly Review in the spring of 1997. The authors claim, "The key rationale for savings that we have reviewed states that households save to prevent future drops in earnings from dramatically reducing their consumption. If the government has a policy that guarantees a certain minimum level of consumption, then those households that foresee that their consumption is likely to remain below the government set minimum have no incentive to accumulate assets. If these people do accumulate assets and their earnings do drop, they will not receive what the government would otherwise have given them..." This reasoning makes it clear that the authors and the audience they are addressing have no real concept of the state of the poor. The suggestion is that poor people make decisions to not accumulate assets based on the largesse they would suppos-edly receive from the government. Hard working families, making wages that can not sustain their lives and the lives of their families, are hardly in the position to make such choices.

No matter what rationale economists or politicians may come up with to explain away this phenomenon, it is an important indicator of just how corrupt the system has become. The extent of this disparity between the haves and the have-nots helps us to better understand the underlying social malaise that has gripped this country. The neo-con-servative ideology is passionately opposed to entitlement programs as exemplified by Social Security, Medicare, and Medicaid etc. Not sur-prisingly, this viewpoint is in accord with business interests that see fantastic potential profits to be made by privatizing these programs. Under the guise of "reform," these programs are currently under assault. In the past, attempts to undermine the fabric of the social safety net have met with strong opposition from the public. However, the George W. Bush administration has proclaimed a state of perpetual war against terrorism, and, in that way, distracted the general popula-tion from its most urgent needs such as health care, employment, housing, infrastructure, etc. Maintaining a heightened and sustained climate of fear among the population has also been used as an effective leverage for the curtailment of civil liberties in the name of security. It is important to note here that while the government is clearly responsi-ble for many of what I maintain are disastrous policies, the methods, tactics and practices that are being employed to expand and solidify power are not significantly divergent from the past. The fault lies not in the individuals who rise to power, but, rather, to the very structure of the institutions that serve the interests of the powerful and serve them exceedingly well.

The extent to which the entrenchment of power and wealth, in the hands of the very few, has impacted a significant part of the population that does not have access to such resources is made evident by studies carried out by the U.S. government. According to the United States Census Bureau Population Report issued in September of 2002, 32.9 million people are below the federal poverty line. The chart below (Chart 4) shows the millions of individuals in poverty represented by non-Hispanic Whites, Blacks and Hispanics out of a total population of 229.9 million.

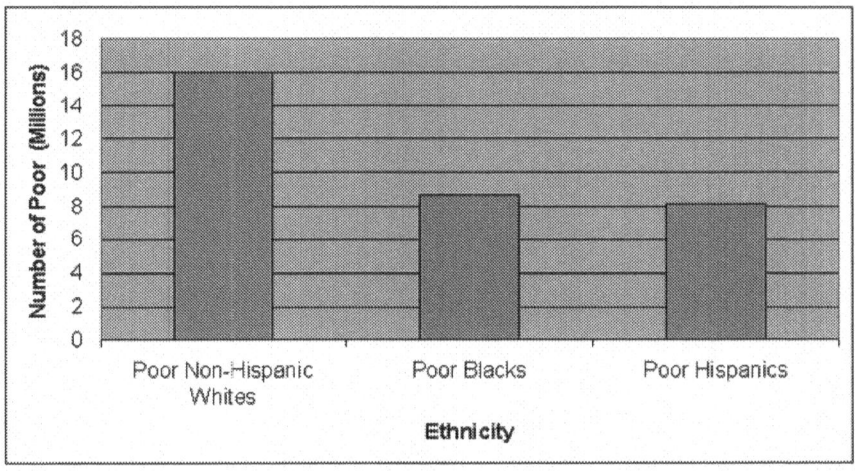

Chart 4 Numbers of the Poor (in Millions) in Relation to Ethnicity

From the data shown below (Chart 5), it can be seen that 7.8 percent of the non-Hispanic White population are poor, while the poverty rate for Blacks and Hispanics are 22.7 and 21.4 percent respectively. This corresponds to 1 out of 5 Blacks and Hispanics living in poverty.

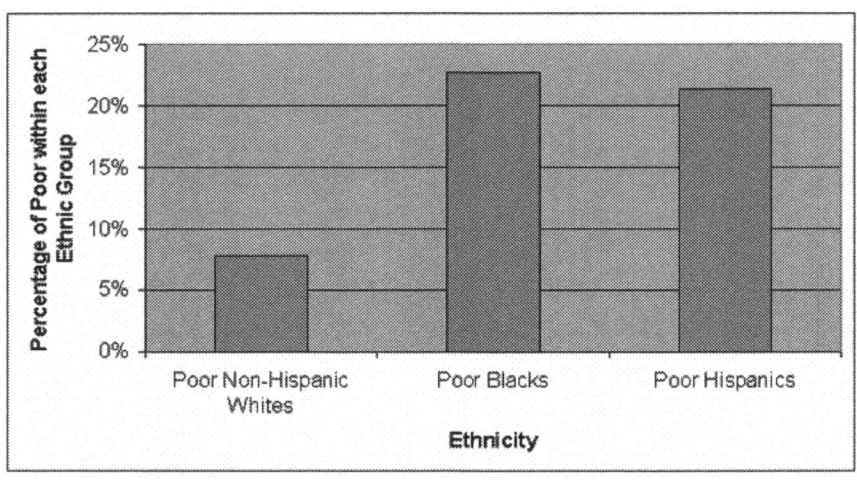

Chart 5 Percentage of the Poor Based on Ethnicity.

In addition, 16.3 percent of the nation's children live in poverty. This represents 35.7 percent of those who are poor. This is quite an extraordinary number since children represent 25 percent of the total population. One must keep in mind that the threshold for poverty is based on an income of $11,859 for two individuals and $18,267 for a family of four. If these figures for income were set realistically in terms of current housing, energy, medical, food and living expenses, the real rate of poverty would probably be considerably higher. Over forty-six million people lack medical insurance and, therefore, access to adequate health care, and this number is growing. Many are homeless. New York, for example, currently (2002) has a homeless population of over 37,000 people, including 4,000 families.

The condition of the poor has been further compromised by the measures imposed by so-called "welfare reform." Many of the states imposed such harsh restrictions on receiving welfare payments, that they have cut the welfare roles by as much as fifty percent.

According to Loretta Schwartz-Nobel in her book entitled, *Growing up Hungry*, the major provisions of the new Welfare to Work legislation reflect changes in public policy that are bound to exacerbate the problems of poverty, hunger and homelessness in America.

Before these changes, the availability of food stamps was based on the need for food. Under the new regulations, food stamps are limited to three months out of every three years for adults under fifty without children, regardless of need. This change no longer protects people from starvation. In addition, the new law precludes those immigrants who are not citizens from obtaining food stamps unless they qualify for specific exemptions.

The law freezes the standard deduction, and lowers the Thrifty Food Plan, which effectively diminishes the availability of food to those most in need. This "reform" effort shifts the administration of the program from the Federal government to the individual states. It is no longer an entitlement program, but subject to states' choices. Aid to Families with Dependent Children (AFDC) has been changed to a block grant referred to as Temporary Assistance for Needy Families (TANF) administered by the states and lacking the guidelines of the old system.

The primary impetus for this reform was the emphasis on work. No genuine effort has been made, however, to focus on training as a way to break the cycle of poverty and dependence. In the Children's Defense Fund study, entitled *Welfare to What?*, it has been shown that many of those forced off of welfare have found themselves working at minimum wage (not a living wage) non-union jobs, often part time, with no benefits available to them. Many are finding themselves without housing. Many of the jobs that welfare clients first accepted proved to be temporary and subject to the vicissitudes of the marketplace. There seems to be no thorough follow up studies of those who have left welfare in order to determine how they have fared in their new economic surroundings.

Welfare reform has created a large supply of surplus unskilled workers to fill minimum wage jobs. This surplus of potential workers guarantees that wages will continue to be suppressed, leaving workers to make due with wholly inadequate incomes. Those who work but are not able to sustain a viable economic life for themselves are now referred to as the working poor.

In Barbara Ehrenreich's thought provoking book, *Nickel and Dimed*, the author, as a journalist, decided to discover first hand what it was like to live on the wages earned from minimum wage jobs. She lived this life in Florida, Maine and Minnesota. On a number of occasions, she found herself needing two jobs to sustain herself. Her experiences demonstrate just what a challenge it is to survive with such employment.

It is not uncommon for a family, in which both parents hold down full time minimum wage jobs, to be unable to pay the rent for the apartment in which they live. In actual fact, it is the minimum wage workers in the U.S. and the factory workers from developing countries who are subsidizing the more well to do by making it possible to purchase products and services cheaply. Such is the nature of the system where the unequal distribution of the wealth is lauded and supported, and the exploitation of the many by the very few is held up a as a successful model for all to follow.

The list below enumerates some additional statistics regarding homelessness, poverty and hunger in America:

- According to the US Department of Health and Human Services, up to 600,000 men, women and children go homeless every night; this number has been estimated to be around 750,000 from other sources

- 1.2 to 2 million people experience homelessness throughout the year

- In a survey of 25 US cities (2000), families with children represent 36 percent of the total homeless population

- New York City has some 37,000 homeless as compared to the 1200 reported in London

- According to the National Coalition for the Homeless, June 2000, the primary causes for homelessness are poverty and lack of affordable housing

- The percentage of poor increased by 41 percent from 1979-1990 where children under 18 represented half that increase

- The median wage required to afford a 2 bedroom apartment is more than twice the minimum wage

- Current TANF benefits and food stamps combined are below the poverty level, i.e. they are inadequate to support a poor family

- The real impact of Welfare to Work has been that only a small fraction of recipients have found jobs that pay above poverty wages. Most new jobs are below the poverty line

- 675,000 individuals lost health insurance in 1997 including 400,000 children

- In 1995-1997, rents increased faster than income for the 20 percent of American households with the lowest income

- Children without a home suffered the highest rates of asthma, ear infections, stomach problems and mental health problems such as anxiety

- Half the children in shelters are under the age of five

- According to the 1996 U.S. conference of Mayors, 19 percent of the homeless are employed

- According to the USDA, 36.2 million Americans live in "food insecure" households (1992), including 12.1 million children under the age of 12

- In 1997, 26 million people secured food through Second Harvest; one third of these were working families and 38 percent were children.

These data do not speak well for the richest nation on the planet. It is indicative of a society that is apparently unwilling to use its immense resources to benefit its own people. Although it may seem to be appropriate policy for those who stand to gain the most from its implementation, in the long run it will prove to be self-destructive. A society that allows so many of its people to suffer needlessly from poverty, hunger and homelessness will find itself depleted of the most important resource of all, the human resource.

If there is any hope of stopping and ultimately reversing this ominous trend, it will come by uncoupling the intimate association between the moneyed interests, as exemplified by corporate power, and the government. Within the current system, big money has undermined truly representative government. Societal problems that require immediate attention, as outlined above, are either worsening from neglect or exacerbated by government policy.

Transformation must also come at the personal level. In a truly great society, all individuals, regardless of ethnic, religious, cultural or economic backgrounds would be treated with care, concern, compassion and respect. This is the goal that we, as a people, should be aspiring to. What is needed is a generosity of spirit and realization that we are all members of a singular species that is currently in a state of crisis on the planet.

5

The Global Economy and the Myth of Free Trade

The economic system based on a neo-liberal capitalistic model is now being actively exported around the world under the mantle of the "global economy." There are a number of international institutions whose reason for being legitimizes this international economy. They are the World Bank, the IMF and the WTO. They seem like mysterious organizations mainly due to the fact that they function in secrecy. All three of these organizations are dominated by the economic might of the United States, and are effective conduits for the propagation of U.S. economic interests.

We will examine these organizations in detail in terms of their makeup, their activities and their intentions, as revealed through their actions. We will look at how their activities have impacted national economies especially in regard to some of the financial disasters that are currently looming in the world.

Janet Thomas in her book, *The Battle in Seattle* refers to the confusing acronyms representing these organizations as an "alphabet soup." It all began in Bretton Woods, New Hampshire in 1944. Economic leaders from the Allied powers met to plan for the aftermath of the Second World War.

The institutions that were created are with us to this day, exerting enormous influence over the economies of the nations of the world. The IMF and the World Bank had their beginnings here. The IMF is a specialized agency whose stated purpose is to stabilize exchange rates and facilitate international trade. Each member of the IMF contributes to the fund in gold and currency. The World Bank is otherwise known as the International Bank for Reconstruction and Development. The Bretton Woods Conference set up the World Bank, the General Agreement on Tariffs and Trade (GATT) and the IMF so that the U.S. dollar would take the place of gold as the medium of international exchange once the war was over, and provide long-term loans to countries devastated by the war.

At that time, capitalism was facing dire prospects. The Allied governments were eviscerated and bankrupt. In addition, there was a power vacuum in those countries that were aligned with or occupied by Germany. The colonial powers (France, England, and the Netherlands) were facing insurgencies in their former colonies. They were in no position to quell these uprisings. In addition, as the Soviet army was sweeping Europe from the East, workers uprisings were occurring as they moved forward. The situation was grim. The United States, on the other hand, not only had been spared the ravages of the war, but had a thriving war industry and had grown quite prosperous. Although it was far richer than all its allies combined, for capitalism to thrive it requires stable governments and markets for its goods. It was, therefore, up to the United States to bring stability to war ravaged Europe and prevent the further spread of the Communist insurgency. The essential ingredient of the Bretton Woods policies was the dollar, which would replace gold and which the U.S. government could print as much as needed. In spite of these policies, Europe was restive. The Soviet army had occupied half of Europe, Tito of Yugoslavia had refused to relinquish power, the Greek civil war was not going well for the Allies and Britain was losing its grip over India.

On March 12, 1947, President Truman invoked what came to be called the Truman Doctrine, which offered aid to the governments of Greece and Turkey and proclaimed an interventionist global role for the United States. On June 5, 1947, Secretary of State George Marshall announced the Marshall Plan, a huge loan program extended to all of Europe. At first, this plan was to include the Soviet Union and Eastern Europe. However, in July of 1947, it was decided that the Soviet Union would get no aid, and that the countries of Eastern Europe were given the choice of either aligning themselves with the United State against the Soviet Union, or be excluded from the Plan and from trading with those countries who would benefit from the loan program. This was essentially the beginning of the Cold War. As a matter fact, the Marshall Plan was used to pressure Britain, France and Italy into rejecting Communism in exchange for assistance.

In 1948, the Italian Communist Party was expected to make important gains in upcoming national elections. This potential outcome was treated with utmost seriousness by the American government. George Keenan, a foreign policy strategist for the government, advocated the U.S. military occupation of the oil fields in Foggia. In an attempt to sabotage the potential triumph of the Italian Communist Party in the election, Allen Dulles, Frank Wisner, James Angleton, William Colby and other key U.S. intelligence officials engineered a strategy that involved financing a campaign of propaganda, sabotage, and secret funding of the Christian Democrats. With the assistance of the Vatican, the Voice of America was used as a very effective conduit of pro-West and anti-Communist propaganda. In addition, the U.S. injected some 350 million dollars into civil and military aid during the campaign. Much of the money used to fund these clandestine activities actually came from captured Nazi assets controlled by the U.S. Treasury's Exchange Stabilization Fund (ESF). This behavior is representative of how foreign policy had become focused on maintaining American predominance in the post-war world.

In response to these unstable conditions and uncertainty about the future, the GATT was created in October, 1947 to ensure the dismantling of trade barriers. GATT together with the World Bank, the IMF and the WTO have become vehicles through which American corporate interests and the multi-nationals maintain economic hegemony by controlling access to natural resources and by dominating the financial markets. Just how do these institutions exert and maintain their influence over much of the world? The best way to answer this question is by example.

The World Bank often lends money to third world countries so that they can use that money to pay corporate interests, from the wealthy nations, to manage and develop large costly projects. The nations that take on this relationship find themselves so deeply in debt that they find it difficult to repay even the interest on their loans. The usual response of the lending institution is to insist that the debtor nation cut back on their social programs. A Structural Adjustment Program (SAP) is often proposed, which basically calls upon the debtor nation to make cuts in programs that benefit the poor, and to privatize industries and services if they expect to receive additional loans to stay afloat. In this way, recipients of these loans effectively relinquish important aspects of their national sovereignty. Nations involved in this scenario, find that they have lost much of their economic base, such as agriculture, that had previously afforded them a modicum of self-sufficiency. Farmers ensnared by this process are often compelled to produce crops for export rather than grow crops such as rice that can feed their families and communities.

An excellent case in point is that of coffee. Coffee is the second largest import after oil, and the United States consumes 20 percent of the world's coffee. The fact is that many small coffee farmers often get prices for their crop that are actually below the cost of production, resulting in an endless cycle of poverty and debt, for they need loans to continue production.

The current situation is particularly ominous, for world coffee prices are at a thirty-year low. The market is severely impacted by overproduction. A reason for this oversupply is that many countries, like Vietnam, now the world's second largest coffee exporter, desperately needing foreign exchange, are forced to sell commodities for export. It has been claimed that the World Bank's loan programs have encouraged the Vietnamese agricultural sector to invest heavily in coffee production. Although there may be no direct link between the World Bank and increased coffee production in Vietnam, the World Bank's policy of promoting the neo-liberal ideology is well known. The overall strategy favors export oriented agriculture that ultimately benefits the privileged class.

The French Development Fund announced a 40 million dollar U.S. loan in 1998 to create 40,000 hectares of arabica coffee in Vietnam. The subsequent dramatic fall in worldwide coffee prices decimated the Vietnamese coffee industry. To give an example of the extent of this decline, the price for a pound of coffee in Vietnam has dropped from over $2.50 in 1963 to about 10 cents per pound in 2002. In Brazil, prices plummeted from about $1.60 a pound in 1986 to 30 cents a pound in 2002.

One of the reasons that a fall in coffee prices has been so devastating to the so-called "Southern countries" is the fact that they have grown dependent upon coffee exports to assuage external debt. Bound by the free trade and investment strategies of the WTO and the structural adjustment programs of the World Bank and the IMF, these countries find themselves obliged to gravitate towards export oriented agriculture in order to repay mounting debts.

In spite of this dramatic drop in coffee prices, the consumer has not seen a comparable decrease in the actual price paid. In fact, the revenues of the major coffee companies has doubled while at the same time the income of ordinary coffee farmers has dropped by over 60 percent according to Nestor Osorio, Executive Director of the International Coffee Organization. This translates into poverty and hunger for thousands of small coffee producers, who are unable to sustain decent living conditions at these prices.

To counter this disturbing trend, there are producers that are adhering to "Fair Trade" practices. Coffee sold under the Fair Trade label must meet certain conditions. Importers must also meet stringent international criteria, one of them being that they must pay a minimum of $1.26 per pound. This minimum price insures that the small coffee grower is at least able to sustain him or herself.

The fair trade coffee alternative also offers the consumer an opportunity to counter the deleterious effects of the global economy. It is an inescapable reality of our times that the cheap labor provided by so many of the world's poor has effectively subsidized the living conditions of the citizens of the wealthier nations. If this troubling relationship is ever to be transformed into a more equitable one, it is up to the average consumer to recognize this reality and alter buying behavior accordingly.

Another example of the real nature of the global economy gravitates around the issues of power generation and dam building in India. This has been brilliantly laid out by Arundhati Roy in her book, *Power Politics* and her essay, *The Greater Common Good.*

In March of 2000, President Clinton visited India. Before that visit, import restrictions on many products were lifted, and contracts worth about 4 billion dollars were signed. Among those trade agreements was a memorandum of intent in regards to a huge hydroelectric dam on the Narmada River as part of the Narmada Valley Development Project that envisions the construction of 3200 dams, thirty of which are to be large dams. This project in the words of Ms. Roy will, "reconstitute the Narmada and her forty-one tributaries into a series of step reservoirs. It will alter the ecology of the entire river basin, affect the lives of about twenty-five million people who live in the valley, and submerge four thousand square kilometers of old-growth, deciduous forest, hundreds of temples, as well as archaeological sites dating back to the Lower Paleolithic Age."

The proposed Makeshwar Dam is a private power project. It is being implemented and sanctioned by the proponents of the global economy. The goal is to privatize the world's water supply. This would effectively take the control of water away from local authorities, and place it in the hands of foreign financial interests, especially those of the United States. An example of such efforts is that of Bolivia in 1999. At that time, Bolivia privatized the public water supply of Cocha-bamba. The company that was slated to be responsible for this privati-zation was a consortium headed by Bechtel, the very same company that has been awarded contracts by the U.S. government for the recon-struction of Iraq. The result of this privatization was a marked increase in the price of water to the point where hundreds of thousands of Bolivians were no longer able to access drinkable water. A strike ensued of such magnitude that in April of 2000 the president of Brazil, Hugo Banzer, declared martial law. Bechtel eventually was forced to flee its offices.

India used to be self-sufficient in regards to power production. Cor-ruption among local officials seems to have played a role in reversing this reality. There is evidence that wholesale theft of power by the industrial sector was implicated in this reversal. The state of Madhya Pradesh, the site of the Makeshwar dam, is now deeply in debt. It has been estimated that about 70 percent of the industrial users steal power in this region.

The Indian government's solution to this problem was to cut agri-cultural subsidies and privatize power production and distribution. Power purchase agreements were made with the now eviscerated Enron Corporation. Enron admitted to paying millions to "educate" Indian politicians and bureaucrats as to the efficacy of such contracts. As it turned out, the power produced by the Enron plant was twice as expensive as the nearest competitor and seven times as expensive as the cheapest power. The efficacy of these contracts with multinationals is to be seriously doubted, since about 70 percent of the rural households in India are without electricity. According to Ms. Roy, "Indian politi-cians have mortgaged their country to the World Bank."

We will now turn our attention to the global economy in another part of the world, South America. In a study compiled by the United Nations Development Program (UNDP) in its annual Human Development Report, the Human Development Index, a measure of quality of life, fell during the first half of the 1990s in twenty of the twenty-four Latin American and Caribbean countries in which IMF policies have been implemented.

The number of people living in extreme poverty in Mexico jumped from 11 to 15.8 million during that period of time. In Chile, 10 percent of the poorest households suffered a decrease of 6.6 percent in income. The most telling statistic of all is the fact that of the forty-three Third World countries, 72 percent experienced an unemployment increase while they were receiving assistance from the IMF.

How is it possible that programs that are supposedly designed to improve the standard of living of the poorest of countries have had precisely the opposite effect? The real purpose of the globalization of trade and commerce is to ensure the dominance and hegemony of the American economy through the activities of the giant conglomerates. We will now examine the policies that are promulgated by the IMF to accomplish this goal.

In the early 1980s Mexico's economy was floundering and sought help from the United States. In return for assistance, the Mexican government was obliged to: privatize state firms, reduce social spending and open domestic markets to foreign trade. Public spending was reduced dramatically, pushing the country into recession. As a result of a massive privatization program, state run industries dropped from 1212 to 448 by December of 1988. By the mid 1980s, Mexico signed on to GATT after intense pressure from the American government and the global financial institutions. Many domestic companies suffered bankruptcy as a direct result of the liberalization of trade. Under pressure from the United States, Mexico amended regulations that formerly prevented majority ownership of domestic industries by foreigners. In 1990, Mexico, under the leadership of Carlos Salinas, pushed for and signed the North American Free Trade Agreement (NAFTA). It was Mexican workers who suffered terribly from these changes. Real wages fell by 30 percent, while the Mexican elite benefited substantially from the neo-liberal economic policies adopted by the Mexican government.

Joseph Stiglitz has become a prominent critic of the IMF, World Bank and the U.S. Treasury. Following a brilliant academic career on the faculties of such renowned institutions as MIT, Yale and Stanford, he joined the Clinton administration as a member of the Council of Economic Advisors. He soon became the Council's Chairman and ultimately, the Chief Economist of the World Bank. Over time, he became disillusioned with the institution's neo-liberal policies and began to voice his concerns. In 1999, he was fired from this organization. The then U.S. Treasury Secretary, Larry Summers, was instrumental in dismissing Stiglitz. It must be remembered that the U.S. Treasury has a 51 percent ownership in the World Bank and, therefore, a controlling interest. Stiglitz detailed the role of the IMF in the Russian loan scandal following the demise of the Soviet Union. On October 10, 2001, he won the Nobel Prize in Economic Science.

From a paper entitled, *Development Policies in a World of Globalization*, Stiglitz writes, "Throughout Latin America today, the question is debated, has globalization failed us or has reform failed? What is clear is that there is disappointment in the policies that have been pushed for the past two decades, the policies focusing on liberalization, privatization, and stabilization which collectively has come to be called the Washington consensus policies. The data for the 90s, the first true test of these policies, when the countries were freed from the shackles of overhanging debt, helps explain the sense of disillusionment. Growth during that decade was just over half of what it was in the pre-reform and pre-crisis decades of the 50's and 60's and 70's. Even in those countries which have seen significant growth, a disproportionate share of the gains have gone to the better off, the upper 30 percent or even the upper 10 percent with many of the poor actually becoming worse off. Little if any progress has been made in reducing inequality, already the highest of any region in the world, and the percentages, let alone numbers, in poverty actually increased."

During his stay at the World Bank, he witnessed the economic crisis in East Asia in 1997 (this will be discussed in more detail later in this chapter). He described this experience in the following way, "...what I saw radically changed my views of both globalization and development. I have written this book (*Globalization and its Discontents*) because while I was at the World Bank, I saw firsthand the devastating effect that globalization can have on developing countries, and especially the poor, within those countries."

According to Stiglitz, when a country gets involved with the IMF, its economy is analyzed and is ultimately presented with a four step program that must be adhered to. These steps are the following: Privatization, Capital Market Liberalization, Market-Based Pricing and Free Trade. They follow a formula that is derived from an ideological perspective rather than from first hand knowledge of the country that is allegedly being helped. An example of how disastrous such policies can be is that of Ethiopia. The IMF insisted that the Ethiopian government undertake capital market liberalization. It wanted Ethiopia to open up its financial markets to Western competition. Of course, impoverished Ethiopia had no way of competing with the large Western banks. At first, Ethiopia resisted, but inevitably gave in. The results were disastrous as could have been easily predicted. When global financial institutions entered the country, it resulted in attracting depositors away from the local bank. These large institutions were much more likely to lend to multi-national corporations then they were to local small business interests. Interest rates rose and the farmers and small businesses were seriously affected. All these factors converged and ultimately had a devastating impact on the Ethiopian economy. This is but another example of the consequences of IMF policies on the poorer nations of the world. Further examples will help dramatize this point.

In August 2001, the economy of Argentina virtually imploded. The policies of the IMF contributed greatly to this disaster. On September 5, 2000, Pedro Pou, the president of the Central Bank of Argentina, signed a Technical Memorandum of Understanding with the IMF. This agreement spelled out the conditions that had to be met before the IMF would help the devastated Argentinean economy. With the country's economy struggling and 20 percent of the labor force in Argentina out of work, the IMF demanded that Argentina cut its deficit from 5.3 to 4.1 billion dollars. Decreasing government spending at a time when the economy is contracting is a recipe for disaster. Unemployment worsened, and to exacerbate the situation further, the IMF insisted that salaries for civil servants and employment programs for the poor be drastically cut, placing an additional burden on the disadvantaged. These policies, once implemented, contributed to the downward spiral in the Gross Domestic Product (GDP) as more and more people could no longer afford to purchase products. At first glance, it might appear that these policies were naive or ill-informed; however, the government was forced to cut expenditures on domestic needs in order to pay the interest on loans to foreign creditors. It is important to keep in mind the close relationship between the IMF and the U.S. Treasury that retains veto power over anything the IMF does. The U.S. is the only country with such veto power. Argentina was desperate for capital, and agreed to these conditions in order to procure a 20 billion dollar loan.

In addition, the IMF also pressured the Argentinean government to liberalize its capital markets. At a time when its economy was spiraling out of control, this liberalization led to currency speculation and the subsequent flight of capital out of the country, as speculators converted their pesos to dollars and shipped the dollars overseas further impoverishing the country, and enriching foreign investors.

The most telling example of how IMF policies have had a devastating effect on the economies of those countries they are supposedly helping is the East Asia economic crisis of 1997. It all began when the Thai baht collapsed. Overnight the Thai currency lost 25 percent of its value. Currency speculation spread through the region affecting Malaysia, Korea, Philippines and Indonesia. The end result was a disastrous depression that endangered regional banks, stock markets and entire economies. It was IMF policies, implemented during such a time of economic uncertainty that dramatically worsened the situation. Joseph Stiglitz states in his book, *Globalization and Its Discontents* that the IMF push for financial and capital market liberalization not only greatly exacerbated the situation, but also played a causal role.

The factors that contributed to this region's economic success prior to the crisis were a high rate of savings and investment. Growth rates had been extraordinary for decades due in large part to high savings, government investment in education and state-directed industrial policy. This progress was made in spite of the pressure from the IMF to conform to Washington Consensus policies that emphasized privatization, and frowned on government involvement in industrial policy. It should be remembered that urging privatization and liberation of capital markets would benefit the Western economies that had the available capital to take advantage of the sale of state owned businesses. Once the crisis was underway; however, the IMF pushed for an even more drastic liberalization of capital markets. Malaysia was one country that bravely resisted the policies of the IMF. Instead, the government tried to keep interest rates low in an attempt to mitigate the flight of capital out of the country. It turns out that Malaysia had a shallow downturn, and was able to recover quickly. We will see exactly how implementing these policies urged by the IMF proved utterly disastrous to other countries in that region.

Thailand is an excellent case in point. Speculation in the financial markets and short-termed indebtedness combined to wreck havoc on the economy. Financial speculators, fearing that the Thailand currency was about to devalue, tried to move out of the currency and convert to dollars. With the practice of free convertibility as condoned by the

IMF, this was easy to do. As the currency was sold on a massive scale, its value plummeted. The government, in an attempt to support its currency, sold dollars from its reserves to buy up its currency, until there were no more dollars to sell. This resulted in the currency falling in value even further. The speculators then moved back into the currency, converting dollars back into the local currency (the baht), and made extraordinary profits.

The IMF, in response to these events, loaned huge sums of money, and according to Stigliz, "The money served another function: it enabled the countries to provide dollars to the firms that had borrowed from Western bankers to repay the loans. It was thus, in part, a bailout for the international banks as much as it was a bailout for the country; the lenders did not have to face the full consequences of having made bad loans." IMF policies, in the final analysis, encouraged capital flight that enriched the already wealthy at the expense of the poor. This policy was mirrored in the economic plight of Mexico in 1994-1995 and Russia in 1998.

Of course, loans to both Mexico and Russia were given under the condition that interest rates and taxes be increased while social spending be reduced. These conditions also included a host of political and economic reforms that effectively usurped the economic sovereignty of these countries and undermined democratic institutions. The net effect of all these policies on the indebted countries of East Asia was a dramatic increase in unemployment, a sharp decrease in the Gross Domestic Product (GDP) and bank closures. The economic plight of those not belonging to the affluent class was devastating.

In regards to IMF policies in Colombia, an article entitled, *IMF Concludes Article IV Consultation with Columbia* was issued by the IMF as Public Information Notice (PIN) No. 99/114. In this publication, the author(s) states, "With regard to other structural reforms, Directors endorse the authorities' plan and policies in the areas of privatization, foreign direct investment, and private sector involvement in infrastructure projects, which hold out the promise of creating a more efficient private-based economy. A few Directors noted that labor market reform was not being vigorously pursued at this time, and urged the authorities to keep this issue on the agenda to help provide further impetus to recovery." This statement clearly exposes the ideological agenda that underlies IMF's policies. The adjustments required of "needy" nations are designed to coerce these nations into imposing neo-liberal economic policies in their countries.

We have examined examples of the perverse logic inherent in the actions of the IMF and World Bank in terms of its attempts to bring economic aid to the developing world. It is clear from these examples that this logic begins to make sense when the real motivations are understood. The policies of these institutions represent a new form of a very old imperialism that exerts its power by coercing the economic, social and political institutions of vulnerable states.

I would like to turn my attention to yet another mechanism through which these institutions operate. According to Vandana Shiva in her book entitled, *Stolen Harvest*, "Trade Related Intellectual Property Rights (TRIPS) calls for a system of uniform patent laws discounting the differing ethical views of much of the developing world, where life is seen as exempt from patenting."

TRIPS was established by the WTO, which was a product of the Uruguay Round of the General Agreement on Tariffs and Trade (GATT). TRIPS was obviously designed to protect Western interests, a contention which is further supported by the fact that U.S. patent laws permit the granting of patents even on discoveries that were made outside of the United States. This has allowed for considerable mischief.

Industrial agriculture, as practiced by the West, pushes for the use of monocultures throughout the world to the exclusion of diverse food crops, animal food sources and the agricultural practices prevalent in societies that are dependent upon this diversity. This is necessitated by the need of agribusiness to control production and distribution of food products. The technologies that are employed to achieve these ends are patents, intellectual property rights and genetic engineering.

To provide a sense of the extent of the concentration of power in agribusiness, ten companies currently control 32 percent of commercial seed and 100 percent of genetically modified seed. These same companies also produce most of the agrochemicals and pesticides for the world market. These conglomerates have been highly influential in shaping the policies of the WTO, which meets in secret and whose policy decisions are purposefully kept from public view. The net effect of both the products of industrial based agribusiness and WTO policies is to flood food exports from the West (the United States and Europe) into the Third World, and to force local economies that do business with the WTO to shift their agriculture from food self sufficiency to the production of foods for export that satisfies the demands of consumers from wealthy nations. This is a strategy that is reminiscent of old style colonialism.

As a result of NAFTA, Mexico imported 43 percent of its food supply in 1996 as compared to 20 percent in 1992, prior to signing this agreement. According to Blanca Velasquez Diaz reporting from the Center for Latin American Studies in an article entitled, *The Economic Consequences of NAFTA: A Labor Organizer's Point of View*, NAFTA has led to an increase in the maquiladoras, assembly plants dedicated to producing products for export to the United States. The wages and working conditions at these plants are deplorable. A more ominous impact of NAFTA is its assault on the democratic institutions of its signatories, including the United States. The Marine Mammal Protection Act required an automatic embargo on yellow fin tuna from those countries that exceeded the U.S. determined dolphin kill limits. This law was designed to protect the dolphin from excessive deaths as a result of being caught in the huge nets used for harvesting tuna. In 1991, Mexico challenged the embargo in a formal complaint against the U.S. under GATT. A panel decided in Mexico's favor, ruling that the protection act violated GATT as a barrier to world trade. The panel ruled that, "…no country may have any law to protect the environment or a species outside its own geographic territory, including the global commons of the oceans and the air or the species inhabiting them, if that law can also affect trade." This is an extraordinary ruling that decided in favor of trade (corporate interests) without regard for the will of the people as expressed by their laws and customs.

In 1991, India agreed to impose trade liberalization on the Indian economy after signing a SAP as part of a loan agreement with the World Bank. The net result of this agreement was a shift from food crop production to cotton for export, using corporate seed. The SAP imposed policies resulted in a decrease in all farm subsidies and reduced India's fiscal deficit. This resulted in a further contraction of the market for farm products and left the country open to cheap imports, cheap imported palm oil being one example. One of the results of these SAPs in India has been an apparent increase in suicides among Indian farmers in the Southern State of Karnataka.

Monsanto is an American corporate conglomerate enterprise that serves as an excellent example of the expansion of corporate power into the global arena. Monsanto, the manufacturer of Agent Orange (the chemical used to decimate the Vietnamese countryside and wreck havoc on the health and well being of both the Vietnamese people and the American troops that fought there), currently controls a large proportion of the seed industry. It has successfully expanded by gaining controlling interests of such companies as Calgene, Agrocetus of W.R. Grace, Asgrow, Holden Seeds, Dekalb and Delta and Pine Land. These acquisitions have given Monsanto an 85 percent share of the U.S. cotton seed market, and a dominant role in the corn market. In addition, it purchased Unilever's European wheat breeding business. The strategy here is to control the genetically engineered wheat market.

Monsanto is a major producer of seed, pesticide, food, pharmaceutical and veterinary products.

To provide insight into the kind of strategies that Monsanto uses in its quest for greater and greater profits, one need only examine its business practices. In March of 1998, the United States Department of Agriculture (USDA) and Delta and Pine Company, a subsidiary of Monsanto, announced a joint patent referred to as the "Control of Plant Gene Expression." This patent permits owners and licensees to create seeds genetically engineered so that the plant's DNA effectively kills its own embryos. Such patents could be applied to all plant species. The perverted logic behind this scheme is to insure that farmers, who attempt to use seeds derived from such genetically engineered plants, will find that these seeds will be unable to grow into mature plants. This effectively wrenches control of the management of seeds and crops out of the farmer's hands and places it under the control of corporate producers.

Another example of this usurpation of local control of agriculture is the so-called "Roundup Ready Gene Agreement" that farmers are compelled to sign if they purchase genetically modified Roundup Ready soybeans. This agreement prevents the farmer from saving seeds or supplying seed to anyone else. This type of contractual arrangement effectively treats living plants, that humans have depended upon for their basic foods for thousands of years, as if they were commodities whose use is licensed and under the perpetual control of corporate interests. All this is done to create markets and maximize profits regardless of the impact on the very essence of human dignity and freedom.

Nowhere in these agreements is Monsanto liable in case of crop failure. It also must be remembered that the real intent of this conglomerate is not to increase the productivity of plant foods, but to increase sales and dependency on its herbicide and pesticide products, for many of these genetically modified organisms are engineered to have an increased resistance to the very products that Monsanto produces: Roundup, a weed control herbicide, being one example.

Much of world agriculture is being directed towards the growth and harvesting of genetically modified monocultures, cotton and soybean being some examples. This strategy threatens diverse ethnic food crops that have sustained human populations over the millennia, and can place the world's food supply at great risk of worldwide devastation by disease or severe climatic change. If the World Bank, IMF and WTO were truly open and democratic institutions, and if the news media were truly informing and educating their audiences, these extreme and self-destructive policies would be under intense scrutiny.

It certainly is not far fetched to see that the underlying intentions behind these corporate policies and practices are the creation and expansion of global markets for products generated by the rich Western nations at the expense of the economies of the developing world. Furthermore, the intent appears to be to deprive small producers in these countries of local autonomy, and to shift production to commodities for export to meet the needs of the world's rich populations. These goals are accomplished through global trade agreements and rules created in secret through instruments such as the World Bank, IMF and WTO.

If the real purpose of the World Bank is to eliminate world poverty and the IMF to ensure economic stability, they have failed miserably. It is time to supplant the world view embodied in these institutions with a different paradigm.

Amartya Sen, a Noble prize laureate in economics, has proposed a different model for economic development. While obviously a proponent of free trade, he envisions a very different approach to its implementation. He identifies the traditional ethics, exemplified in the policies of the IMF and World Bank, as focusing on the primacy of income and wealth. Furthermore, he defines poverty as a "deprivation of elementary capabilities which can lead to premature mortality, illiteracy and other consequences."

In his book, *Development as Freedom*, he postulates a freedom based orientation to policies geared towards economic development. The author claims that, "With adequate social opportunities, individuals can effectively shape their own destiny and help each other. They need not be seen primarily as passive recipients of cunning development programs."

This different perspective allows application not only to developing countries but also to the developed world. The fact that tens of millions of Americans lack access to adequate health care provides a striking example. A link between income and mortality can also be readily established. The life expectancy of African Americans compares to poor countries such as China, Sri Lanka, Jamaica and Costa Rica.

In this view of development, a consideration of personal liberties can not be divorced from economic consequences. The link between income and poverty is, of course, self evident. Freedom can be seen not only as residing in so-called political freedoms, i.e. freedom of speech and freedom of assembly, but also dependent on those aspects of economic life that are fundamental to living successfully, i.e. adequate health care, housing and food, referred to as substantive freedoms. What good are political freedoms to those who expend all their energy simply trying to survive?

In this paradigm, development is seen in terms of substantive freedoms and requires an analysis of the unfreedoms that people may suffer. This differs substantially from the current operational approach of the traditional institutions. As we have seen from previous examples, the IMF's approach to economic development often exacerbates, or, in extreme cases, creates the very inequities that make the plight of the poor even more devastating.

Global economic institutions have evolved into huge secret beauacracies that serve the interests of the powerful. Over time, the policies that have been promulgated, under the guise of economic development, have inspired the development of wide spread resistance around the world, as exemplified by the growing power of so-called Non-governmental Organizations (NGOs).

During the Ninth Plenary meeting of the Fifty-seventh General Assembly, Timothy Harris, Minister for Foreign Affairs and Education of Saint Kitts and Nevis, said, "We call on the United Nations to facilitate, develop and promote mechanisms where partnership, collective responsibility and mutual respect are allowed to flourish." He stated that the operating principle of globalization should be to level the playing field so that equal opportunities were available to all nations. It is only when the hungry are fed, the vulnerable made strong and the disenfranchised are empowered that the world can be freed of anarchy, terrorism and conflict.

It is essential that there be a sustained demonstration of disapproval of neo-liberal policies regarding global trade, especially from the American public, if there is to be any hope of the transformation of these policies into reasoned, sustainable and humane alternatives. This is especially important, since these same policies have dramatically impacted American workers and their families for the worse.

6

The Myth of Empire

It would be mistaken to presume that the concept of an American empire is a wholly new one. In the early nineteenth century, nations in Central and South America were beginning to free themselves from Spanish imperialism. The United States government had its eye on these countries and, under the leadership of President Monroe, issued the Monroe Doctrine in 1823. The doctrine served notice to overseas powers that Latin America was under the American sphere of influence. The successful war with Mexico in 1854 resulted in the addition of the territories of California and the Southwest to the American real estate. During the remaining years of the nineteenth century, there were many instances of militaristic adventurism on the part of the United States government. These are documented in Howard Zinn's *A People's History of the United States.* They involved military expeditions against countries like Argentina, Nicaragua, Japan, Ryukyu and Bonin Islands, Uruguay, China, Angola, Portuguese West Africa and Hawaii.

By 1890, the Native American population had been subdued, contained and subjugated. Following the severe economic depression of 1893, there was a move to find foreign markets for American made goods. This certainly set the stage for America's involvement in the Spanish American War, and the subsequent acquisition of the Philippines, Puerto Rico and Cuba acquired through force of arms.

Many Americans were troubled with the nation's imperialistic designs. Notable among them was Mark Twain, who was vehemently opposed to the Philippine-American War. He served as vice president of the Anti-Imperialist League during that time. In a letter written to Joseph H. Twichell on January 10, 1901, he wrote, "…This nation is like all others that have been spewed upon the earth—ready to shout for any cause that will tickle its vanity or fill its pocket. What a hell of a heaven it will be, when they get all these hypocrites assembled there!

"You are supposing that I am supposing that I am moved by the Large Patriotism, and that I am distressed because our President has blundered up to his neck in the Philippine mess; and that I am grieved because this great big ignorant nation, which doesn't know even the A B C facts of the Philippine episode, is in disgrace before the sarcastic world—drop that idea! I care nothing for the rest—I am only distressed and troubled because I am befouled by these things."

On April 2, 1917, President Woodrow Wilson appeared before Congress and requested a declaration of war against Imperial Germany. In November of the same year, the Bolshevik revolution changed the political landscape. The U.S. had placed its hopes on the Provisional Government that ultimately was to fall to the Bolsheviks. On November 11, 1917, the Russian ambassador to the United States, Bakhmetev, declared that he would not accept the authority of the newly installed Bolshevik regime. Bakhmetev ultimately became, in fact, an agent of the U.S. government. Lenin was determined to get Russia out of the war and eventually made a separate peace with Germany embodied in the Brest-Litovsk Treaty. This treaty threatened to jeopardize the Allied war effort. This taken together with the anti-capitalist doctrine of the Bolsheviks convinced President Wilson to authorize a secret war against the Russian government. The plan was to join Japanese forces in Vladivostok, Siberia. This strategy obviously did not succeed, for the Bolsheviks remained in power. The United States has repeatedly attempted to intervene in the domestic affairs of sovereign nations whenever it felt its own interests at stake. The arrogance of power that is so evident in contemporary American foreign policy is nothing terribly new.

Following World War II, the United States effectively supplanted Great Britain as the major imperialist power embracing the capitalist model of economic development. Throughout this recent history, corporate power has gained greater and greater ascendancy. In this model, progress is seen as a relentless production of new products, and of securing and maintaining market share for these products. This pursuit of ever increasing productivity requires prodigious amounts of energy and resources. The fact that Americans consume 40 percent of the world's resources while they constitute only 5 percent of the world's population is a testament to this analysis.

The United States has been engaged in many conflicts (as detailed earlier) that have been associated, one way or the other, with this quest for energy and resources. In order to maintain its ascendancy, the foreign policy of the United States has been geared to control the political and economic direction of a good part of the world. In addition to brute military force, many other means are at its disposal, the most effective being the corrupting influence of money. The IMF, the World Bank, the WTO and the financial markets are some of the means by which the democratic evolution of other cultures has been successfully thwarted. The policies of these institutions, under the guise of promoting a global economy, often lead to the establishment of political oligarchies populated by members of the affluent classes and possessing the trappings of democracy but not its substance. The sum total of these activities can be equated with imperialism at the service of furthering the goals of empire.

What makes the activities of the George W. Bush regime so troubling is the extremist ideological view upon which all of its policies are formulated. Bush is rooted in a Christian fundamentalism that has an essentially myopic view of existence, and sees the world in stark black and white terms. There is no gray as far as he is concerned. It is important to remember that his frame of reference is severely limited by how little he does read. He is surrounded by advisers and colleagues that share the same ideology, and effectively filter out any information that does not conform to his understanding. It is, of course, very convenient that the world that he sees is divided into good and evil camps; the United States is not only on the "good" side, but it is also represented as the moral leader of all the countries that align themselves in this way. He has become, in his own eyes, a kind of new world messiah and emperor. This way of thinking ignores the real nature of human culture and society, and wholly rejects the lessons that can be learned from history. This fundamentalist view of the world and its people is essentially irrational and terribly dangerous. George W. Bush is an ideologue, and, for this reason, is a cause for concern.

Beneath the ideological rationalizations for extremist policies, there exists quite a different set of interests. George W., his family, his colleagues and friends have benefited directly and substantially from the policies initiated by both himself and his father. The involvement of George Bush Sr. in the Carlyle group has been discussed previously. The corporate interests that have benefited greatly from the government contracts awarded them for the reconstruction of Iraq have been major contributors to the Bush 2004 presidential campaign fund that is predicted to reach 200 million dollars.

In addition, George W. Bush's economic ties to the Saudi government has resurfaced especially in regard to the events immediately following September 11. There is also additional evidence that he depended upon Saudi investors to salvage some of his business ventures when he was dabbling in the oil industry as a younger man. It is a considerable coincidence that the world view he embraces, brings to him, his friends and family such substantial financial rewards.

The fact that he sees the policies of the United States as representative of a moral universe, in spite of the real cost in human lives that these policies have wrought throughout the world suggests either an extraordinary dissociation from reality, or a deep and underlying cynicism. I suspect that his extreme ideological constructs prevent him from acknowledging the real nature of power and its consequences in the world.

I would further suggest that this right wing ideology and will to power is what motivated George W., with the help of his brother Jeb, to engineer the fraud that took place at the Florida polls on Election Day 2000. The extent of this fraud is so extraordinary that I will now detail the actual events that stole an election.

Thanks to the brilliant investigative reporting of Greg Palast, as described in his book, *The Best Democracy Money Can Buy*, it is clear that there was a list of registered voters, who were supposedly accused of felonies in the state of Florida, which was used to bar many individuals from voting. According to Florida law, a person convicted of a felony no longer has the right to vote. This list had over 57,000 names on it. It has been shown that a large number of names on the list were fraudulent, i.e. people were on the list who had no felony convictions. A majority of individuals on the list were African American. Even though the state paid over two million dollars to ChoicePoint, the company that compiled the data, state officials required only an eighty percent match when validating the names on the list. This produced an extraordinary large margin of error that resulted in the exclusion of many voters from casting their ballots even though they were innocent of any felony.

There were an additional 40,000 names of individuals that had committed felonies in other states and had served their time before moving to Florida. According to a decision that had been made in the Florida courts, such individuals could not be barred from voting. The Florida administration, under Jeb Bush, ignored this decision and used this list to strip additional individuals from the voting roles. This was a blatantly illegal act.

Furthermore, machines that counted the ballots throughout the state were equipped with the optional capability of rejecting ballots that were erroneously completed. In representative counties with a majority of white voters, this option was turned on, allowing the voters to correct their ballots and re-submit them. In counties where the majority of voters were African American, however, this option was often not implemented, increasing the likelihood that black voters would have their votes rejected if the ballots were improperly filled out.

All this evidence points to a massive fraud perpetrated by the administration of Jeb Bush, and to the fact that Al Gore did indeed win the state of Florida and the election. Once this successful coup had taken place with the help of the Supreme Court, George W. Bush put together an administration whose members shared the same neo-conservative beliefs, and were prepared to take the entire country down a path leading to the establishment of the American empire or what they chose to call: "The New American Century."

The extremist policies of this administration buoyed up by the calamity of September 11, have effectively ceded greater control of American life to corporate interests. Many of the serious social ills confronting the American people have been greatly exacerbated by the Bush administration. Included in this list are: homelessness, poverty especially among children, health care, the crumbling infrastructure, a growing prison population, the deleterious affects of global warming, air and water quality, the increasing numbers of working poor and unemployment. These problems are of serious proportion, yet they have been effectively ignored by the administration and the Congress.

In terms of the domestic policy promulgated by the Bush administration from its very beginnings, there has been a gradual and inexorable dismantling or diminishing of a large body of environmental regulations: the Clean Air and Water Act, the Endangered Species Act, the acceptable level of arsenic in the water, the acceptable level of mercury in the environment and many other examples, which are outlined in Jim Hightower's book entitled, *Thieves in High Places*.

One of his first acts as President was to rescind work place ergonomic regulations designed to protect workers from suffering workplace injuries. His administration effectively undermined the efficacy of the Kyoto treaty by refusing to become a signatory. This treaty was designed to set international limits on the production of greenhouse gases so as to reduce the deleterious effects of global warming. Since the U.S. burns so much fossil fuel, the main culprit in the production of greenhouse gases, its refusal to participate effectively undermines the goals of the international effort.

Major legislative initiatives proposed by the government have been clearly aligned with business interests. In many cases the legislation itself has been crafted with the help of the very industries that would directly benefit from its passage. The formulation of energy policy and the subsequent passage of the so-called Energy Reform Bill exemplify this fact, as described earlier in this book.

During George W. Bush's tenure, there has been a steady erosion of civil liberties within the United States beginning with the passage of the Patriot Act, as outlined previously, enacted under the shadow of the supposed war against terrorism. A war that the leadership claims is a perpetual one. Under that banner, we have witnessed the expansion of the military budget to some 500 billion dollars, staggering deficits and the worsening of living conditions for a majority of Americans. The call to patriotism has been cynically manipulated since September 11 in order to implement a broad range of policies that effectively cede greater and greater power to the corporate class. This has been demonstrated by repeated attempts to privatize social programs such as Medicare and Social Security; a strategy that is completely analogous to the strategy that the IMF imposes on nations that receive its "help."

The great danger that the George W. Bush administration poses is not its will to empire, per se, but that it hopes to effectively complete the transfer of power from the people to those who possess the wealth, and, therefore, to unravel the remaining remnants of true democracy in favor of an oligarchy. If this trend continues, we will be faced with a society where the gap between the rich and poor widens, where personal freedoms are relinquished, where the nation is faced with a culture of perpetual warfare and where there is no social agenda to alleviate and correct serious social issues within the society.

The U.S. Nobel Laureate for Economics George A. Akerlof made the following statement, "I think this is the worst government the U.S. has ever had in its more than 200 years of history. It has engaged in extraordinarily irresponsible policies not only in foreign and economic but also in social and environmental policy. This is not normal government policy. Now is the time for people to engage in civil disobedience."

In my estimation, this is a very dangerous path we are on. This nation seems to live behind a veil of ignorance and isolation overshadowed by an image of itself that is essentially delusional. The myths that perpetuate these misconceptions must be discarded so that all of the nation's people have a real chance at shaping their own destinies.

7

Conclusion

The United States is at an important juncture in its short and illustrious history. Over two hundred years ago, the colonialists had successfully wrestled independence from the British. The republic that supplanted foreign rule was crafted with high expectations of creating a viable, stable and independent state. Although revolutionary in concept and ideals, the architecture of the new government continued to be based upon rule by the wealthy and elitist class.

Throughout its subsequent history, there were many occasions when the opportunity arose to establish a truly progressive and free society in which the voice of the people could be heard. In each case, the established power managed to reassert its authority often with the overt use of force. The eras that come to mind are the post Civil War era after the emancipation of the slaves, the progressive labor movement in the 1930s and the civil rights movement in the 1960s. State power was effectively used in these times of social unrest to thwart real change, as described earlier.

The country, with its wealth of natural resources, expansive frontiers and diverse populations, has always been endowed with great potential. The vitality of the American economic engine is indicative of that potential. The possibilities inherent in the American nation are being squandered, however, by both the delusion and arrogance of power. Since the end of World War II, the United States became a world leader, and as a result of the collapse of the Soviet Union, became the world's only super power. The power and potency of the alleged American empire is being trumpeted by the government. This particular government is made up of men who represent the needs, aspirations and ambitions of the wealthy. In their eyes, the world and its people, including American citizens, are seen as imminently exploitable. They, like many who have preceded them, regard the free and vital political expression of the vast majority of people, many who lead marginal lives, as a threat to their authority. To ensure a "stable" world, any real movement for a change in the political, social and economic order must be thwarted. The members of Congress, whose supposed role is to represent the people, have themselves been corrupted by both power and the corporate interests that they have become dependent upon. Although this is not a new scenario, the unabated continuation of the status quo will most likely lead to tragic consequences especially for the American people, for the following reasons.

The dependence upon the force of arms as a legitimate tool for achieving political goals has left the nation with a staggering budget deficit, an expanding national debt and a continued erosion of the good will of vast numbers of people throughout the world, who have come to see the United States as exceedingly dangerous.

The health and well being of the American people is further exacerbated by the subservience of government to corporate power leading to unconscionable tax cuts for the wealthy, a steady deterioration of environmental safeguards and a contraction of social services for those in need. Working people have paid a huge price for the ascendance of corporate power through the permanent loss of jobs that actually pay a living wage.

The significant reduction of the national budget in those areas that encompass social programs has essentially put tens of millions of people at serious risk. A substantial portion of the population, as detailed earlier, already lacks accessibility to health care, adequate nutrition, education and housing.

If these policies continue unabated, the outcome is not hard to imagine. The two-tier economic structure will become more entrenched, leaving larger and larger numbers of people without any hope of improving their plight. The quality of air, water, soil and oceans will worsen. The deplorable condition of the nation's inner cities will continue to be neglected. More prisons will be built to house the underclass and the disadvantaged. The numbers of people who are homeless, or live with hunger, or who are one paycheck away from falling into an economic abyss, will get larger.

Many domestic issues that require immediate attention have been effectively sidelined, ostensibly to focus national energy and resources on the current war against terror. The response of those in power to this singular threat against their authority and economic hegemony throughout the world is to retaliate against the enemy with overwhelming force. In other words, terror is fought with much greater terror. As we have seen in the many examples cited regarding the use of American military power, the underlying motivation for such action is to enforce a kind of stability that ensures American economic domination regardless of the cost in human life. We have seen the implications of the use of such an arrogant and mindless use of power: many parts of the world have come to view the United States as brutal, unscrupulous and inherently dangerous. To many, we have become a pariah nation. Many previous empires in human history have taken the same path, and, in each case, it has ultimately led to grief.

How can this kind of future be avoided? Meaningful change will not come about by fiat or violent revolution. In the history of nations, revolution from the top has invariably meant the replacement of one elitist class by another. Real and effective change must proceed from the collective energy of the people. Change will happen incrementally as more and more citizens recognize the nature of the threat and take upon themselves the responsibility to demand and precipitate change. There are, in fact, many organizations in place that represent a diversity of interest groups that are involved in issues such as poverty, homelessness health care and the environment. As of yet, these organizations have not had enough of a following to provide the momentum for real change to occur.

Individuals need to be awakened to the stark reality that faces them. The machinery of propaganda is effectively used by the private media and government to delude the public and obfuscate the truth. The myths that are perpetuated to benefit the ruling class appeal to the need to belong and to feel a part of something great.

There has been, however, a slow and inexorable movement towards exposing these falsehoods for what they are. More and more voices are calling for the uncoupling of corporate interests and government through such vehicles as campaign finance reform. Many are supporting a more equitable distribution of wealth through a major restructuring of the tax code. Many diverse organizations are actively advocating substantial changes in public policy that would make health care available to all and end homelessness and hunger in this country. There are those who are dedicated to exposing the real nature and consequences of the global economy as crafted by the powerful.

If a meaningful re-organization of the social order is to occur, basic changes in attitude and understanding must happen first. This country has the potential to build a true democracy in which freedom is not merely an option available only to the wealthy. It is time to break free from the archaic ideas of government and power and enter into a new covenant where all life is respected, cherished and allowed to reach its fullest potential. It is time for the myths that obscure our potential as a people, to be replaced with a new reality. We, as a people, are at a crucial juncture. Collectively, the future is in our hands.

Notes

Introduction

"USA Patriot Act," Electronic Privacy Information Center
Nat Henthoff, "Vanishing Liberties," Village Voice, April 11, 2003
William Rehnquist, "All the Laws but One: Civil Liberties in Wartime", Knopf/Vintage, 1998
"The State of Civil Liberties One Year Later," Center for Constitutional Rights

Chapter One: The Myths of Democracy and Freedom

Charles Beard, "An Economic Interpretation of the Constitution," Princeton University Press, 1956
Alexander Hamilton, "The Federalist No. 9 and Federalist No. 35"
Thomas Jefferson, "Letter to James Madison," January 30, 1787
Vincenzo Quadrini, Jose-Victor Rios Rull, "Understanding the U.S. Distribution of Wealth," Federal Reserve Bank of Minneapolis Quarterly Review, Vol. 21, No. 2, Spring 1997, pp 22-36

Chapter Two: The Myth of Equal Justice

Bob Woodruff, "The Prison Boom, Number of Prisoners Has Doubled in Past 12 Years," ABCnews.com, March 15, 1999
"Disproportionate Share of Prison Inmates Are Black," Associated Press, July 18, 2001
Barnett R Rubin, "The Political Economy of War and Peace in Afghanistan," June, 1999

Chapter Three: The Myth of the World Policeman

Noam Chomsky, "American Power and the New Mandarins," The New Press, 1969

Chris Hedges, "War is a Force that Gives Us Meaning," Public Affairs, 2002

Noam Chomsky, "Understanding Power the Indispensable Chomsky," The New Press, 2002

Walter Wink, "The Powers that Be Theology for a New Millennium," Galilee Doubleday, 1998

"The Essays of A.J. Muste Edited by Nat Handoff," Bobbs-Merrill Company, 1967

Noam Chomsky, "Rogue States," South End Press, 2000

Howard Zinn, "A People's History of the United States," Perennial Classics, 1999

Kermit Roosevelt, "Countercoup: The Struggle for Control in Iran," McGraw Hill, 1979

Robert J Maddox, "The Unknown War with Russia," Presidio Press, 1977

Kendrick A. Clements, "The Presidency of Woodrow Wilson," University Press of Kansas, 1992

Gabriel Kolko, "The Politics of War: The World and United States Foreign Policy 1943-1945," New York: Pantheon, 1990

Filicity Arbuthnot, Rosalie Bertell, Ray Bristow, Peter Diehl, Dan Fahvey, Hank van der Keur, Daniel Robicheau, "Depleted Uranium a Post War Disaster for Environment and Health," Laka Foundation, May, 1999

HJ Wingender, HJ Becker, J Doran, "Study on depleted uranium(tails) and on uranium residues from reprocessing with respect to quantities, characteristics, storage, possible disposal routes and radiation exposures," European Commission(Ed.), Eur 15032, ISBN 92-826-6478-3, Luxembourg, 1994

AK Gupta, "Energy Futures Oil," Commentary Online, November 2002 Vol 15 Number 11

Thalif Deen, "Middle East There's No Business like War Business," Asia Times Online, April 4, 2003

Noam Chomsky, "Rogue States the Rule of Force in World Affairs," South End Press, 2000

"Bush Praises Sharon's Pullout Proposal," World, April 15, 2004

Jules Witcover, "Congress Should Remember Lessons of Tonkin," Baltimore Sun, September 23, 2002

I Michael Heyman, "Statement of Michael Heyman Secretary of the Smithsonian Institution," January 30, 1995

Kai Birw, "Silencing History," The Nation, February 20, 1995

Edward Spannaus, "When U.S. Joint Chiefs Planned Terror Attack on America," Executive Intelligence Review, October 12, 2001

Patrick Keaney, "Columbia's 'dirty war'," Phoenix.com, December 19, 2002

Testimony by John J Maresca Vice President, International Relations, Unocal Corporation, "House Committee on International Relations Subcommittee on Asia and the Pacific," February 12, 1998

Oliver Burkeman and Julian Borger, "The Ex-President's Club," The Guardian, October 31, 2001

"The Secret CIA History of the Iran Coup," 1953

"London Draft of TPAJAX Operational Plan,"

"National Security Archive Electronic Briefing Book NO. 28"

Masuji Ibuse, "Black Rain,", Bantam Books, 1985

Christopher Hitchins, "The Trial of Henry Kissinger," Verso Press, 2001

"National Security Archive Electronic Briefing Bank No 4," CIA archives

Naomi Klein, "Iraq is not America's to Sell," Guardian Unlimited, November 7, 2003

Pillsbury Winthrop LLP, "Reconstruction of Iraq Coalition Provisional Authority Issues Order Number 39 Allowing Foreign Investment in Iraq," International Trade News Brief, September 23, 2003

Ian McWilliam, "Central Asia Pipeline Deal Signed," BBC News, December 27, 2002

Chapter Four: Free Enterprise and the Myth of Prosperity

Kevin Phillips, "Arrogant Capital," Little Brown and Company, 1994
Ben H Bagdikian, "the Media Monopoly," Beacon Press, 2000
Kevin Phillips, "Wealth and Democracy," Broadway Books, 2002
Jim Hightower, "Thieves in High Places," Viking Press, 2003
Lorestta Schwartz—Nobel, "Growing Up Empty, The Hunger Epidemic in America," HarperCollins Publishers, 2002
Children's Defense Fund, National Coalition for the Homeless, "Welfare to What?" 1998
Barbara Ehrenreich, "Nickel and Dimed," Henry Holt and Company LLC, 2001
Arianna Huffington, "Pigs at the Trough," Crown Publishers, 2003
United States Department of Commerce, Bureau of Economic Analysis, "1998 Country Report on Economic Policy and Trade Practices: Columbia," 1998
International Monetary Fund, "IMF Concludes Article IV Consultation with Columbia," Notice (PIN) No. 99/114, December 29, 1999
U.S. Department of Commerce Donald L. Evans Secretary, "Poverty in the United States: 2001," September 2002

Chapter Five: The Global Economy and the Myth of Free Trade

Arundhati Roy, "Power Politics," Second End Press, 2001
Arundhati Roy, "The Greater Common Good," Modern Library, 1999
Vandana Shiva, "Biopiracy," South End Press, 1977
Janet Thomas, "The Battle in Seattle," Fulcrum Publishing, 2000
Joseph E Stiglitz, "Globalization and Its Discontents," W.W Norton and Company, 2003
Amartya Sen, "Development as Freedom," Anchor Books, 1999

Blanca Velasquez Diaz, "The Economic Consequences of NAFTA: A Labor Organizer's Point of View," Center for Latin American Studies, 2002

Mark Tully, "Hunger Drives India's Farmers to Edge," CNN, 2001

Martin, Hart and Landsberg, "Challenging Neoliberal Myths, A Critical Look at the Mexican Experience," Monthly Review Organic Consumers Association, December 2002.

"The First Full Account of America's Recruitment of Nazis, and its Disastrous Effect on our Domestic and Foreign Policy," Blowback, 1988 www.mosquitonet.com

Timothy Harris, Minister for Foreign Affairs and Education of Saint Kitts and Nevis, 9th Plenary meeting of the Fifty-seventh General Assembly, 2002

Chapter Six: The Myth of Empire

Michael Moore, "Stupid White Men," Regan Books, 2201

Greg Plast, "The Best Democracy Money Can Buy," A Plume Book, 2003

"Text on the Marshall Plan Speech," State Department Version, June 4, 1947.

"U.S. Nobel Laureate Slams Bush Gov't as Worst in American History," Der Spiegel Magazine, July 29, 2003

"Anti-Imperialism in the United States 1898-1935," Edited by Jim Zwick,

Index

0-595-32691-9